A ROOM OF HER OWN

A ROOM OF HER OWN

INSIDE THE HOMES AND LIVES OF CREATIVE WOMEN

• ROBYN LEA •

· INTRODUCTION ·

In the infancy of the 21st century, a new kind of woman has claimed her rightful place on the world stage. Part creative philosopher and part rebel, she is a trailblazer who refuses to compartmentalise, neglect or render impotent any of her talents or interests. Instead, her entire life is a canvas for her artistry. We see it in her home and studio, on her table and in her wardrobe, and in the poetry she brings to her relationships. Now more than ever, we need to turn our gaze to the light of this woman of courage and grace, whose example offers us a new way forward. Not on the mercenary and unsustainable path that has led the planet to the edge of a dangerous precipice, but one that honours art, life, beauty and the human spirit and benefits the Earth and all of humanity.

This book features twenty of these extraordinary women and takes us across the world on a private tour into their personal and professional domains. Among them are painters, sculptors, writers, chefs, designers, jewellers, curators, makers and directors, though none of them can be defined by just one discipline or job title. While they are generally of European heritage and living in Western countries, I hope that their stories and philosophies will inspire women everywhere.

Each woman has navigated a unique path, though they are united in their reluctance to play by the rules of others. A number of them have experienced societal pressure and institutional bias that have worked against women to various degrees since time immemorial. Several have also lived through traumatic personal experiences on the road to self-fulfilment. Instead of turning away from the darkness, however, they have chosen the often-difficult path of self-exploration, involving an uncompromising search for answers to a series of important questions: Can I work through pain from my past then transform it into a positive energy source that feeds my creativity, spirit and wellbeing? What self-defeating or destructive thoughts are holding me back from reaching my full potential and enjoying a life of great purpose and meaning? Am I completely honest about my feelings, needs and dreams? What should I let go of in order to simplify my life, quieten the noise and exist in harmony with my clan, my work and Mother Earth?

These questions arise in a moment of cultural contemplation, a kind of 'New Renaissance', and while it is difficult to predict whether it will have the lasting impact and influence of the original Renaissance in Europe of the 14th–16th centuries, they share several important features. Both movements emerged in the context of widespread social, political and economic change precipitated by devastating pandemics, which led to periods of heartbreak, turmoil and individual and collective soul-searching. Just as the spread of the COVID-19 virus in 2020 was hastened by the ease of global travel, the Black Death of the 1300s quickly extended across Europe and beyond, thanks to the expansion of land and sea trade routes to the Near and Far East, to devastating effect. In turn, a rare opportunity arose to overhaul dysfunctional systems and questionable ethics and attitudes and replace them with a society based on humanist values.

It was against a backdrop of violence, fear and instability that Cosimo de' Medici (1389–1464) came to power in Florence. He brought to his role a great passion for literature, antiquity, philosophy, philanthropy, art, architecture and business. And a love of humanity.

— **PAGES 2–3**
Fiona Corsini's Florentine sitting room, with a collection of artworks by Fiona and her friends lining the wooden console.

— **PREVIOUS**
Poppies in artist Claire Basler's studio in France.

— **OPPOSITE**
Fiona Corsini at Villa Le Corte, home to her brother's family. The coat of arms represents the Corsini family on the left and the Trentinaglia family on the right.

— OPPOSITE
Interior of fashion designer Lucilla Bonaccorsi Beccaria's apartment in Milan.

Cosimo's extraordinary cultural legacy was built upon further by his grandson Lorenzo 'the Magnificent' (1449–1492), who became the figurehead of the most significant cultural, artistic and intellectual rebirth since Roman times. In the same way that today we see a deep yearning for meaning and purpose beyond status and consumerism, Lorenzo envisaged a world of social harmony where the human spirit and human achievements would soar.

The progressive and often altruistic ideals he stood for were shared widely thanks to the invention of Gutenberg's commercial printing press in 1450. With millions of low-cost books available in Europe for the first time, new ideas were broadly disseminated and the world became ripe for more than merely cosmetic change. Prefiguring the effects of the digital revolution today, this seismic shift in communication during the Renaissance gave voice and prominence to previously marginalised or invisible individuals and groups. Access to the written word, which had been monopolised by religious, noble and often tyrannical leaders until the 14th century, was now also in the hands of the people. Social mobility became more common as power structures shifted, and the absolute authority of the Catholic Church was questioned in favour of secularism. Recognising the implications, Renaissance leaders stepped into the vacuum and seized the opportunity to publish and widely distribute their discoveries, theses and doctrines. Such visions of a more beautiful world helped quell the chaos, elevate the lived experience of millions of people and lead Europe out of the medieval era and into a brighter future.

While the impact of the Renaissance period resonates with and informs us to this day, its rich offerings remained largely unavailable to women of that time, who were only permitted to observe from the sidelines. Their voices were rarely heard in the public sphere, their presence was allowed in few schools, their opinions were not sought in important matters and their work was almost never seen on the walls of the castles, cathedrals and palaces of Europe. In all but the rarest of cases, their artistry lay dormant and lifeless through lack of oxygen.

Now, more than 500 years later, the work of women creators, thinkers, makers and innovators is being showcased on new platforms to the benefit of all. We are witnessing a much-needed democratisation of the worlds of art, fashion, film, music and design. This new era has amplified the voices not only of women of exceptional talent and artistry like those in these pages, but of billions of women whose previously invisible professional and domestic lives are being shared in the public sphere for the first time in history. The blurring of boundaries between private and public, immediate family and global online communities, art and life, is once again setting the stage for change, but this time the views and work of women can no longer be easily sidelined or ignored. The immediacy of the connection between creator and collector, philosopher and follower, mentor and student, designer and buyer makes it possible for more women to sidestep the patriarchal structures of the past. Instead, they can now establish their own global platforms and find buyers and supporters for their work.

The creators and pioneers in this book hail from eight different countries and many different backgrounds, but share a drive to infuse all aspects of their lives with their creativity. Several among them inherited powerful artistic legacies from their forebears that they then reshaped and built upon to satisfy their own values and ideals. Others have lovingly coaxed an artistic life from the remnants of families displaced or destroyed.

While many of the women would not identify themselves as leaders, it is impossible not to consider them so when we immerse ourselves in the colour and brilliance of their lives. Emblazoned on the walls of their homes, the hues on their palettes or plates and the prints and patterns on their gowns, coats and capes are the markings of artists and thinkers that the world needs like never before. These are women who strive for the best in themselves while simultaneously lifting our spirits, encouraging our dreams, feeding our hearts and showing us a better future.

† † †

· AUSTRIA ·

ALICE STORI LIECHTENSTEIN

· DESIGN CURATOR ·

When the topic was first raised in 2004, Italian design curator Alice Stori Liechtenstein dismissed the idea of moving into her husband's Austrian castle, Schloss Hollenegg. It was an unexpected decision, given the home's fifty-two rooms, 16th-century Renaissance courtyards and recorded history dating back to 1163. Not even the grand staterooms with their beautifully preserved frescoes, rare ancient tapestries and gilt-framed royal portraits could tempt Alice to change her mind. It took eleven years and a thoroughly modern plan for her to reconsider.

Alice was born in Milan and grew up in the northern Italian city of Bologna. Her mother, Marina Deserti, runs a company importing gourmet food, premium teas, champagne and fine wines. Alice's father, Gabriele Stori, was an art critic, dealer and collector. Though he died in a car accident when she was just two years old, Alice got to know him through stories her mother shared. 'She told me he was great with art and had a really good eye, but was terrible with money.' Reputedly a charming man, he had a deep knowledge of and affinity for art and supported and maintained close friendships with several significant Italian artists of the 1960s and 70s. Alice also learned about his tastes and personal preferences through the paintings he collected, which hung in the monochrome interiors of her childhood home. Works by the postmodernist painter and filmmaker Mario Schifano, conceptual artist Alighiero Boetti, sculptor Mario Ceroli and Italo-Argentine artist and theorist Lucio Fontana are the cornerstones of the collection.

Alice pursued a degree in design and interior architecture at the European Institute of Design in Milan. Her graduate thesis was supervised by Alessandro Guerriero, one of the founders of influential avant-garde design group Studio Alchimia. 'From Guerriero, I learned to build a story behind even the most mundane of objects, to search for a philosophy, to look beyond the material,' Alice says. After graduating, she worked with Guerriero and other influential designers at Radiosity in Milan on projects for the Triennale di Milano design museum, and helped to create the influential online design, art and fashion company Yoox – 'I started as the girl who could use AutoCAD, and left as project manager.' After completing a master's degree in design of public spaces at ELISAVA in Barcelona, she was ready to launch a career as an independent design curator. But first, she needed a holiday.

A friend from Milan had invited her to join a two-week sailing trip around the Greek islands. Alice found herself increasingly drawn to the vessel's skipper, Alfred, a self-contained man with strawberry blond hair: 'I liked the fact that he did not speak much, but when he did, he never said anything stupid. He seemed so grounded, even at sea, and had so much authority without seemingly trying.' Later, Alice was surprised to learn that the object of her affections was otherwise known as Prince Alfred Paolo von und zu Liechtenstein. Three years earlier, at age twenty-six, he had inherited Schloss Hollenegg, a castle in the Austrian countryside. Alfred's ancestor Johann I Joseph, Prince of Liechtenstein, bought the estate in 1821, along with eleven other significant properties in the region, for his son Prince Franz de Paula of Liechtenstein.

Alice and Alfred married in 2005. However, the castle's isolated rural location, three hours south of Vienna, meant she could not imagine herself making a home there. 'I could just never see myself living in that kind of setting, sitting on a velvet sofa or taking long walks in the countryside,' she explains. So, they lived instead about an hour away in Graz, which has the advantage of an international airport, ensuring easy access to Alice's projects in Venice, Milan and Paris.

— OPENING IMAGE
Alice Stori Liechtenstein at home in Schloss Hollenegg.

— OPPOSITE
The Red Gobelin Room with floor rug by Odd Matter, designed for the 2018 exhibition *Legacy*.

Alice threw herself into Austrian life, which included lecturing for the master's degree program in exhibition design at Graz's FH Joanneum university, establishing a local design business and writing a design blog. Slowly, things began to change. She added German to her long list of languages, started to feel a part of the local design community, developed a network of local friends and had three children. However, juggling family life with frequent travel for work, lecturing and running her business began to take its toll and she yearned for a simpler life. She came up with a plan: given various practical impediments to moving the family away from Austria to one of the epicentres of the contemporary design world, why not move into the castle and invite the design world there?

In 2014, the family relocated to Schloss Hollenegg. Soon after, Alice established the non-profit 'Schloss Hollenegg for Design' to support research, development and understanding of design. The concept came from a simple idea: 'I suddenly realised that when you mix the old and the new, it's much more exciting. The aim was to try to get modern elements into each room.' Such unexpected juxtapositions would heighten the impact of both the contemporary design works and the ancient settings.

Just as Alice learned how to interpret design years ago in Milan, she now helps others to do so: 'It's really important to me to teach people how to interpret objects, to understand how things are made and why they're made in that way — not just how to use them, but to ask "What's the meaning behind them?"' Every year, different rooms of the castle are opened for a design exhibition. Annual themes are like chapter headings in Alice's own personal story and relate to her experiences living in the castle. For the first year, in 2016, she chose the theme 'slow', reflecting the pace of her new rural life and the challenge of transitioning away from the constant flow of stimuli in her previous one. She used yoga and meditation to help her adjust, which she had practised in Milan years prior.

For Alice, the benefits of slowing down outweigh the disadvantages: 'We need to remind ourselves that certain processes — advanced thinking among them — require time to mature and develop.' The *Slow* exhibition, which included works by mischer'traxler, Dean Brown and Dossofiorito, among others, offered the viewer an opportunity for thoughtful contemplation. 'By presenting objects that force us to reconsider our perception of time — to sit, observe, think — it is perhaps possible to offer a new, more positive reading of dilatoriness,' Alice wrote in the exhibition catalogue.

Despite her undeniable good fortune in life, Alice has also dealt with loss and tragedy, with the premature death of her father and, in 2016, the death of her brother — her only sibling. She keeps perspective by focusing on the positive aspects of her life and by placing equal value on her mental and physical health: 'Look ahead, stay busy, work, have fun, dance, keep your friends close by and limit contact with toxic people.'

Curation is the vehicle by which Alice has chosen both to learn and to teach: 'For me, curation is like writing a book, telling a story or making a film. It's about the experience. It's about suspending your disbelief for an hour or two, like when you immerse yourself in a film at the cinema.' In the short time since Schloss Hollenegg for Design was established in 2015, the program has grown in scope and influence, helping Alice achieve her vision of the castle as a global design destination. It has also allowed her to continue her father's legacy and develop an inspired vision for her children and future generations. Alice believes that as humans, 'we have an inherent urge to create and make, and are continually, and often inadvertently, building a legacy that will outlive our physical existence.'

Design has helped Alice immerse herself in the rooms and history of the castle. It has also been the catalyst for opening the castle to the general public for the first time since the Middle Ages, when villagers lived inside its fortified walls. She has achieved her goals by trusting her professional and personal instincts and by honouring her needs as a creative thinker. In doing so, she has developed a stimulating environment not just for her family but also for the local community, the broader public and the global design world.

† † †

— The Blue Room,
featuring a
neo-Gothic
four-poster bed.

— OPPOSITE
Velvet-covered
neo-Gothic furniture
and 17th-century
Brussels tapestries
in one of the
castle's bedrooms.

— OPPOSITE
Drawing room with early
18th-century hand-painted
Chinese wallpaper and an
Achille and Pier Giacomo
Castiglione Arco floor lamp.

— ABOVE
The ritual of family meals
inspired the 2019 exhibition
theme, *Ad Mensam* (Latin for
'at the table').

— FOLLOWING
The Baroque drawing room
with contemporary aluminium
chairs by OS&OOS created for
the 2019 *Ad Mensam* exhibition.

21

— ABOVE
Marble bust depicting Princess
Therese of Liechtenstein in the
Great Hall.

— OPPOSITE
Renaissance stairway leading
to the residential wing of
the castle.

— OPPOSITE
An ornate late-Renaissance carved doorframe in the west side corridor.

— ABOVE
Traditional architecture contrasts with contemporary design; these pieces were installed in the west side corridor for the 2019 *Ad Mensam* exhibition.

— CLOCKWISE FROM
TOP LEFT

– Still-life with fabric,
treasures and curiosities found
throughout the castle.

– Still-life with objects found
in the castle's ancient rooms.

– The vaulted ceiling in
the office space provided
inspiration for Belgium-born
designer Nel Verbeke's
'The Architecture of a Tea
Ceremony' concept.

– Detail of one of the castle's
neo-Gothic rooms, with black
inlaid furniture.

– The south corridor behind
the castle's Baroque church
offers spectacular views.

– Drawing room detail.

– Detail of family dining room.

– Detail of the sideboard
in the family dining room.

· MILAN ·

MARTA FERRI

· FASHION DESIGNER ·

M

ilan-based fashion designer Marta Ferri not only embodies modern Milanese style herself but offers her clients made-to-measure dresses, coats, pants and gowns that marry old-world style with a future-forward attitude.

Her creations are known for their unique patterns and colours, though her own childhood wardrobe was surprisingly devoid of both. Her mother, Barbara Frua De Angeli, a respected rug and interior designer who possesses the understated personal style typical of many Milanese women, enforced a preference for monochromatic or muted tones with few patterns.

In contrast, the interior of Marta's childhood home in Milan was rich in vibrant colours and textures. Barbara used her considerable aesthetic skills to tell visual stories in each room, paying particular attention to the employment of light and shadow as tools to establish specific moods. Despite providing little freedom for the young Marta to select her own clothes, Barbara encouraged her to decorate her bedroom however she pleased. Marta still treasures her early memories of choosing her first wallpaper, which featured a green vine pattern.

When Marta was four, a new annual rhythm was established where she would spend school terms with her mother in Milan and holiday periods with her father, Fabrizio Ferri, a globally renowned photographer who is also a composer, author, set designer and film director, either in New York or roaming the world. When she was with her father, different rules applied: 'With him I was free to choose whatever I wanted to wear, so it was like a bomb of colour. I remember going to the mall and choosing brightly coloured towels and bathers, then travelling around the desert with him in a motor home where he was shooting on location, wearing bright colours and sunglasses and drinking Coca-Cola through a straw. I felt like I was in paradise.'

In 1991, when Marta was seven, her father established Industria in New York City's West Village. Modelled on a thriving business he had founded in Milan in the 1980s, it contained a series of large studios for hire along with equipment, post-production facilities, staff capable of handling every aspect of a photographic shoot, and a casual Italian eatery. It soon became the leading full-service studio facility in Manhattan, attracting photographers such as Annie Leibovitz and Peter Lindbergh, and clients including Gucci and Louis Vuitton.

After finishing high school, Marta worked in a Milanese fabric boutique for a year, before relocating to New York where she was offered a job at Industria. Although she was the daughter of the owner, Marta was required to earn her stripes through self-discipline and hard work, like all the other staff, working as an assistant, set designer, photo retoucher and producer.

During her time in the United States, Marta started dating her future husband, Carlo Borromeo, who was studying in San Francisco at the time. Despite their budding romance, however, Marta applied for a job at Prada and at the age of twenty-four began travelling the world as part of its visual merchandising team.

After eighteen months on the road, Marta was ready to explore her long-held dream of working for herself. She planned to become a jewellery designer, and having had some wonderful experiences with Carlo in Argentina, where his family had a home, they decided to start there, each quitting their jobs. However, it wasn't to be. With the encouragement of her future mother-in-law, Paola Marzotto, Marta had been designing her own clothes to wear at events and women had begun inquiring about her designs. Marta convinced Carlo they should stay in Milan after all, so she could establish her own fashion label.

— OPENING IMAGE
Marta Ferri in the private Palazzo Borromeo courtyard adjacent to her atelier in Milan, wearing a dress of her own design.

— OPPOSITE
Behind the scenes in Marta's atelier in Milan, with made-to-order pieces in various stages of development.

In 2009, Marta opened her first atelier in a small, disused apartment space adjacent to the home she shared with Carlo in Milan's historic centre. After painting the interior like a circus tent in pink and grey stripes and installing furniture, including a sewing table, she was soon receiving clients by appointment. She began ordering sumptuous fabrics from around Europe and sourcing historic and vintage textiles that were no longer in production, and a specialist tailor was employed to sew each garment to her specifications.

Marta brings an instinctive and decisive approach to the design of her bespoke pieces. During the first client meeting, measurements are taken and all the requisite details are noted, including the date and format of the upcoming event and the client's favourite colours. Marta intuitively gleans other information, such as the client's unique personal traits. Then, like a chef creating a dish, she begins with the most vital ingredient – the fabric: 'Once a client falls in love with a fabric, the design is born from that material.' Silhouettes are discussed, designs are drawn up and the first fitting takes place within days.

Marta enjoys creating pieces for women of all shapes and ages. She urges her clients to forget about what other people think and likes to infuse both the process and the designs with an element of fun. She says, 'While it is important to wear something appropriate for your age and for the event, in the end I encourage them to do whatever they feel like. I ask, "Do you feel comfortable in it? Do you feel beautiful in it?" and if they answer yes, then that's what is essential.'

Marta followed the same 'Do whatever makes you feel good' philosophy in decorating the three-storey home she shares with Carlo and their two children. Located a short walk from her atelier, the heritage-listed house features a mix of contemporary and antique furniture and objects. Entering at street level, you are greeted by a leafy courtyard. Upstairs, the immense first-floor living room is bathed in natural light thanks to its corner location and large windows. Furnishings include heirloom pieces from her grandmother's home in Liguria and twin wicker chaises longues from the Borromeo family's Sardinian estate. Teak boards salvaged from a former school in India line the floor.

Marta has had several important role models in her life, including her mother and mother-in-law, who both encouraged her early interest in fashion design. The depth and breadth of Marta's informal training, coupled with a strong instinct for design and innate personal style, have earned her the title of a world-class designer.

† † †

— PREVIOUS
The living room, showcasing a suite of deep olive velvet 'Paul' sofas designed by Vincent Van Duysen and Gio Ponti armchairs in a vivid tangerine fabric of Marta's choosing.

— OPPOSITE
Marta's office in her atelier.

— ABOVE
Living room corner with
Fornasetti lamp and a
collection of mounted stone,
marble and crystal spheres.

— OPPOSITE
The games room, with a feature
wall covered in silverware
design drawings.

— FOLLOWING
A pair of matching wicker
chaises, classical wooden
columns and a salvaged wood
floor give warmth and
personality to the light-filled
sitting area.

38

— CLOCKWISE FROM
BOTTOM LEFT

— Detail of the atelier
workroom, showing pins
and ribbons.

— Dresses on a rack in
the atelier.

— Still-life with a collection
of objects and materials
found in the atelier.

— The atelier's fabric remnant
cupboard.

— Marta wearing one of
her designs.

— Detail of Marta's pinboard
in her Milan office.

43

· MILAN ·

JJ MARTIN

· FASHION & HOMEWARES
DESIGNER ·

H

idden within trauma and grief is a doorway that can lead to personal transformation. Finding the entry point requires the courage, curiosity, intelligence and flexibility to wade wide-eyed into dark waters, where the seed of change resides. When discovered and nurtured, this seed has the power to emerge from the quagmire like a lotus flower, changing the individual forever.

'Your pain and suffering are the keys to opening up your greatest potential,' explains California-born, Milan-based fashion, jewellery and homewares designer JJ Martin. Central to her creative, spiritual, psychological and (sometimes punishing) physical journey has been her courage to listen for, then plunge into the depths of, her most uncomfortable emotions.

So, when JJ found herself in pandemic-induced isolation crying face down on the kitchen floor of her new, as-yet-unfurnished apartment for the third time in as many weeks, she did not shy away from her anguish. Recently separated from her husband of fifteen years and with her Milan store and showroom shuttered, the shift from her very public and lauded roles as founder, designer and 'Chief Spiritual Officer' of her company, La DoubleJ, to seclusion was confronting. Yet JJ welcomed the opportunity for introspection, seeing in it a chance to 'plant the seeds for another way of being, another way of tending to my own inner garden, another way of growing new gardens'.

In many ways, JJ had been in training for this moment for years. In the twelve months leading up to the lockdown, she embarked on a number of solo pilgrimages deep into the Javanese jungle that, in her words, 'turned me inwards and turned on the rest of my being: the physical, the emotional, the spiritual, the energetic'. It was there, in the solitude of the wilderness, that she found clarity. While 'moving with the Earth's natural rhythms', she felt a powerful spiritual shift, and some of the pieces of her personal puzzle 'began to fit together to create a beautiful mosaic'.

The experience provided a stark counterpoint to her life in Milan, which, despite a daily two-hour practice of yoga and meditation, was overflowing with 'noise, food, conversations, busyness and really big lists'. Added to her own expectations were those of the fashion world: to look good, produce prolifically, evolve creatively, promote the brand abroad, deliver orders on time, be seen at the right parties and, when in attendance, be beautifully dressed and fabulous company. In short, it was exhausting and meant she was hardly ever truly alone.

To fully appreciate the significance of JJ's personal transformation, it helps to understand where she came from. JJ grew up in the Pacific Palisades, Los Angeles, and camping, fishing, hunting and hiking were the order of the day in her outdoorsy family. But with an action-man father and a mother who was 'a doer, not a feeler', JJ's emotional development was thwarted by 'a set of invisible fears: a fear of negative emotions, a fear of being weak and vulnerable, a fear of being judged'. Feeling disconnected, she developed protective emotional armour and powered through the first two decades of her life wearing it. With her emotions and untapped creativity buried deep inside, she was unprepared for what was to come.

Two years after JJ left home for college, when she was just twenty, her father died. With few tools to navigate her grief or address other traumas from childhood and adolescence, she sought therapy, was diagnosed with clinical depression and was prescribed antidepressants. But after seeing a series of psychiatrists, she became disillusioned, abandoned the treatments and relocated to San Francisco, then New York City three years later.

— **OPENING IMAGE**
JJ Martin, wearing a La DoubleJ *Paloma* dress, in front of a pair of 1940s still-life paintings by her great-grandmother, Swedish artist Katrina Van Ike.

— **OPPOSITE**
La DoubleJ *Tree of Life* wallpaper, designed by Kirsten Synge, with custom-made Deruta vases and a charger plate sitting on an Italian vintage bamboo table in the foreground.

— OPPOSITE
**Custom-made table set with
La DoubleJ tableware and
linen napkins.**

JJ landed in New York in 1998 – the same year the television series *Sex and the City* was launched. On paper, she exemplified the sort of woman fictionalised on the program. With an acerbic wit, a gift for erudite storytelling and a west-coast-meets-east-coast style perfectly suited to her marketing role at Calvin Klein, she was the epitome of glamour and success. Other aspects of her life in the Big Apple, however, were not so picture-perfect. She lived in a shoebox-sized apartment, ran through snow, rain, hail or humidity for an hour at 6 am every day to keep her demons at bay, wore her armour from dawn to dusk and never took a break. A tiny clue to another way of being was offered to her during her first-ever yoga class: 'I remember at the end of the class, when it was dark, I completely broke down because it was the first time I'd really slowed down.'

At age twenty-eight, after meeting Italian entrepreneur Andrea Ciccoli at a party, JJ relocated to Milan to live with him. It took years to fully adjust, as everything was different – from business etiquette and notions of acceptable attire to rules of social engagement and typical work hours, not to mention the language. Eventually, JJ emerged as a top fashion and design writer and contributing editor for publications such as *Harper's Bazaar* and *Wallpaper**.

In 2005 JJ and Andrea married, and for the next six years JJ danced to a vigorously pulsating work and social schedule while trying to get pregnant. With no success, she embarked on a series of IVF treatments over many years that resulted in the 'emotionally, psychologically and physically destabilising' loss of three pregnancies. After abandoning IVF in 2013 along with her hopes for biological children, she recognised her need to process the loss and pain and address unresolved past traumas.

This time, she sought help not from traditional medical practitioners but from a wide range of healers, teachers and guides. A Native American Eagle Woman in Hollywood told her to slow down 'so her soul could catch up', and made her aware of the damage done when she judged herself and others too harshly. A white witch in Scotland explained the various levels of human existence and urged her to honour and mourn for her lost pregnancies. A blind Theta healer in rural Italy helped her understand the benefits of her empathic abilities and taught her the importance of connecting with her father's spirit. JJ also used shamanic massage to awaken the feminine energy in her body and qi gong treatments to clear 'internal blocks, piles of pain and recurring rivers of fear'.

Interestingly, it was a naturopath who guided her on a philosophical path. He shared stories about the ancient Greek goddesses and helped her reframe her experiences through an understanding of archetypes. He told JJ that she wasn't depressed, but simply needed to get in touch with her inner Persephone, whose story of psychological transformation – learning to exist in darkness and emerging from it wiser and more powerful – could help her deal with her past. In goddesses such as Demeter, Athena, Artemis and Aphrodite, JJ saw her own strengths and weakness and was able to draw on their narratives to help maintain balance in her own life. Later, they also inspired one of her fashion and homeware collections. 'The goddesses are one of the many portals that a woman can use to access deeper levels of her consciousness,' she says. 'They can shine light on her behaviour, on recurring themes, on strengths and weaknesses. The stories of the goddesses don't need to be taken literally. They are reminders of universal patterns that females engage with.'

The combined effect of all JJ's learning was that she felt safe enough to take off her armour and step into her powerful, vulnerable, open, authentic self. She let go of past traumas, became more compassionate with herself and with others, and embraced a broader understanding of fertility. Whatever the goal, she says, 'the brief is the same: women are natural-born creators. New life can blossom in our hands, eyes, hearts or stomachs – but it all starts from the womb, the second chakra. And you absolutely must create a fertile environment for yourself for the creativity to flow.'

† † †

— OPPOSITE
Guest room detail.

— ABOVE
Tulips in a La DoubleJ *Wildbird*
bubble vase.

51

— JJ's bathroom wall displays her vintage necklace collection.

— OPPPOSITE
A mid-1800s Tibetan altar creates a focal point for JJ's daily spiritual practice. 'Creativity is an outward expression of what's happening in an inner world,' she says. 'So the inner world has to be honoured.'

— FOLLOWING FROM LEFT
— Sitting room with a mix of custom-made and vintage furniture.

— Mirrored sideboard with glass objects by Matteo Thun, La DoubleJ and Tapio Wirkkala.

— CLOCKWISE FROM BOTTOM LEFT

— JJ's sitting room, with mid-century furniture and La DoubleJ vases.

— Exterior of JJ's apartment in Milan.

— Model wearing a La DoubleJ *City Coat* with *Carnevale* print.

— La DoubleJ plates and napkins from the *Pavone* and *Poesie* series.

— A peek behind velvet curtains into JJ's wardrobe.

— Model wearing a La DoubleJ *Long Fancy* dress in silk twill.

· NEW YORK ·

LISBETH McCOY

· ARTIST ·

There was a quietness in the childhood of artist Lisbeth McCoy. With no siblings and a father who was often abroad for work, she lived with her mother in an old two-storey red-brick house in a small village on the Danish island of Funen, which at the time was only accessible by boat.

The influence of Lisbeth's early life remains a constant in her current art practice, which encompasses sculpture, installation, painting and mixed media. Like a meditative antidote to modern-day ailments, her art invites the viewer to be still. The evocative figures she creates stand around her homes and studio like clay characters in a silent film, while cut-paper mobiles move almost imperceptibly in softly lit corners. The whispering visual stories are told in a restrained, almost monochromatic palette, interrupted occasionally by vivid red or tangerine accents.

In some ways her early childhood, which centred around her mother, was idyllic. 'I don't think my mother knew she was an artist – but I think she was,' Lisbeth says. Her mother's creativity was woven like a magical thread through every aspect of their daily lives. Coming downstairs in the morning, Lisbeth would find her nestled in a chair drinking tea from one of their large handmade ceramic cups. Painted with black stripes and deep-red rosehips, the cups had been made in Jutland by one of her mother's favourite artisans. The very same shade of red appeared in her rosehip jam, which was made in batches each summer. At Christmas time, during long walks, they gathered twigs and leaves from the forest to make decorations, and handmade paper cut-outs dressed their windows and tree.

Lisbeth's relationship with her father, however, was tempered by his absences. Despite training as a teacher, his true passion and talent lay in hairdressing and he worked as an international hairstylist. When he was home, Lisbeth would watch as he practised new styles on her mother, and his love of sculptural contours, using hair as his medium, was something that Lisbeth came to appreciate as she grew older: 'When I started studying art, I always thought of him because I realised that while he wasn't taught to be an artist, he really was an artist. So we became much closer when I started art school.'

A few months after Lisbeth's fourteenth birthday, her mother died from cancer at the age of forty-four. Her death was a severe shock, coming just weeks after her diagnosis. Undeterred, her father continued his work commitments away from home, leaving Lisbeth for long periods to fend for herself. No avenue, professional or otherwise, was provided for her to grieve. She tried her best to continue her daily routines, though much had changed. While school was unavoidable, other things suffered and she stopped ballet and horseriding.

At age nineteen, against the wishes of her father, who wanted her to attend a local university, Lisbeth relocated to Paris, where she was scouted by a modelling agency. Her first job was one of the most esteemed assignments in Paris at the time: a six-month contract as an haute couture model for the House of Chanel. It was while living in Paris that Lisbeth took her first steps towards grieving her mother, and the following decade was a period of searching and experimentation. After five years of modelling she turned to acting, and in 1989 moved to New York to study at the American Academy of Dramatic Arts, then spent several years pursuing film roles in Los Angeles.

Next, partly as a reaction against big-city life and the values espoused by Hollywood film studios, she moved to a remote property in the Australian outback, where she lived in a Victorian-era homestead. Out in the Australian bush she moved another step closer to healing, by reconnecting with nature and riding horses again, and the vast, dry plains of the outback were added to her growing catalogue of inner landscapes.

After hopscotching through a series of interconnected adventures, Lisbeth began to channel her energy into sculpture. Like rediscovering a language from childhood, it felt

— OPENING IMAGE
Lisbeth in her Tribeca studio, with her work *Untitled I*, 2016, displayed in the foreground.

— OPPOSITE
Lisbeth by the Susquehanna River at the Cooperstown property she owns with her husband, gallerist Jason McCoy.

— OPPOSITE
A light-filled reading corner in Lisbeth's Tribeca studio.

— FOLLOWING
The circular dining room in Lisbeth and husband Jason McCoy's New York City apartment.

familiar and natural. The work allows her to channel her feeling for nature, build on her love of drawing and delve into her personal narrative. Memories of her mother inform her work, as does the work of artists such as Louise Bourgeois, Barbara Hepworth and Eva Hesse.

Lisbeth's studio in Tribeca has large arched windows on two sides, ensuring it is awash with natural light. When she found it in 2011, she knew immediately it was right. She stripped the space back to a shell and added natural wood tables, linen-backed chairs and workstations for paper or clay. 'The interior and the work go hand in hand,' she says. 'I like to arrange things in a certain way, and that has to do with spatial issues between the elements. That becomes the composition, and the composition sometimes becomes the work.'

In another step towards healing, Lisbeth recommenced ballet and dance classes, and resurrected music as an important part of her life and work. In the studio she mostly listens to jazz: 'I can walk into my studio and think, "I just don't know how to get going today", and so I put on music, move some furniture and do a few dance steps. It releases me and gets me out of my head.' Intuition guides her creative process and, like jazz, she is happily led down improvised paths and welcomes the work that appears in the process.

After a day in the studio, Lisbeth heads uptown to her apartment in the Ansonia building, on the Upper West Side. Unsurprisingly, given her embrace of the French capital in her early adult life, the apartment appears more typical of Paris than New York. Shared with her gallerist husband, Jason McCoy, and their teenage son, Charles, the apartment is a haven: 'Apart from dance, my meditation is to be in my home moving furniture around to make compositional arrangements … like a collage.' One of the features of the apartment is a circular dining room with hardwood herringbone floors and views through original iron-framed windows. Mid-century Danish furniture is dotted throughout, working in harmony with 20th-century artworks. Lisbeth's drawings are framed in natural wood and her sculptures are displayed on white plinths in the dining room. Everything is considered, from the natural fibres that cover the beds, floors and furniture to the balance of furniture in each room.

Whenever practical, Lisbeth and her family escape to their holiday house, Byberry Cottage, a Gothic Revival house in Cooperstown, Upstate New York. Fearing it would be torn down, they bought it in 2018 and began a thorough restoration, redoing the foundations, lifting the ceilings, painting the walls and installing a traditional Danish fireplace in the kitchen. They also repaired a small boatshed and deck on the banks of the Susquehanna River, accessed via a winding, tree-lined dirt path.

As she sits quietly with a large teacup on the deck by the river, or stands gazing out at the water, Lisbeth looks like a woman at the height of her powers. She has created a universe of beauty and meaning for herself, her husband and their child, just as her mother did for her. She has also found the inner confidence and emotional clarity required to express, through her work, the vulnerability and frailty that links us all.

† † †

ON BECOMING AN ARTIST:
ISAMU NOGUCHI
AND HIS CONTEMPORARIES,
1922–1960

GREENE
STREET

— OPPOSITE
Dressing table in Byberry Cottage's master bedroom.

— BELOW
Exterior, Byberry Cottage. In saving their Cooperstown home from demolition, they also preserved a small part of local history. The two-storey building was constructed in 1855 for author, naturalist and philanthropist Susan Fenimore Cooper. Her father, James Fenimore Cooper, was an esteemed author whose works included *The Last of the Mohicans*, and her grandfather was the town's founder, William Cooper.

— OPPOSITE
The living room of Lisbeth and her husband Jason McCoy's New York apartment, with early and mid-20th-century furniture, two encaustic paintings and a cast-iron sculpture by Martin Kline and a wooden sculpture by Sidney Geist.

— BELOW
New York City dining room detail with painting by Nicholas Wilder; Model PK22 canvas chairs by Poul Kjaerholm, produced by Kold Christensen; Zanotta side table with bronze bowl/sculpture by John Pawson; and the hanging sculpture *Bumppo I*, 2017, by Lisbeth McCoy.

— OPPOSITE
Byberry Cottage kitchen.

— BELOW
The master bedroom of the
New York City apartment.

72

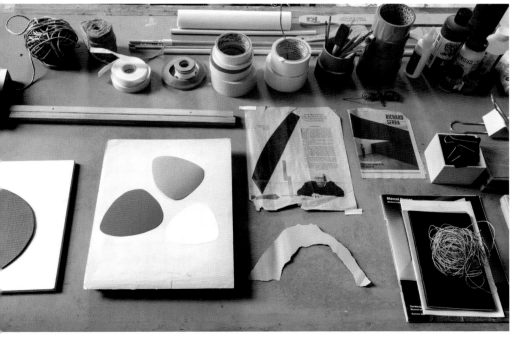

— CLOCKWISE FROM
BOTTOM LEFT

— Cooktop and copper pots
in the Byberry Cottage kitchen.

— View from the New York City
dining room.

— Fired clay head by an
unknown Danish artist on
a sideboard in the master
bedroom in New York City.

— Master bedroom detail,
Byberry Cottage, Cooperstown.

— Materials and works in
progress in Lisbeth's
Tribeca studio.

— View of the studio with
Lisbeth's hanging works
and sculptures.

— Work table in the studio.

— Lisbeth McCoy, *Head of
Young Boy*, 2014; made with
plaster and wax.

73

· FLORENCE ·
· SICILY ·

FIONA CORSINI
DI SAN GIULIANO

· ARTIST ·

As the early morning light rises over the citrus grove of their Sicilian farm, artist Fiona Corsini sweeps her hair into a loose bun, pinning it with three silk flowers in a row across the back of her head. Two blood-red blooms frame the third flower in the centre, a shade of bridesmaid pink – somehow hopeful. She wears them each day, not only for adornment but to honour and keep close people she has loved and lost, and as a reminder of life's fragility and beauty.

Unharried and thoughtful, she seems like a woman of another time. And in many ways, she is. Born in 1969 in Florence to Princess Giorgiana Corsini and Prince Filippo Corsini, she grew up in the ancient hilltop village of Barberino Val d'Elsa in Chianti, located about a half-hour's drive south of Florence. Closed to traffic, its streets are devoid of many modern intrusions. The sights, sounds and scents of her childhood were much the same as they had been centuries prior, when her ancestors walked the same medieval paths.

Village life had a happy predictability. Fiona attended the nearby school, had long lunches at home and went on adventures in the surrounding hills with her twin sister, Nencia. They foraged for wild asparagus, climbed trees in the orchards and took part in the annual grape and olive harvests. Painting was another favourite activity, encouraged by their maternal grandmother, Elizabeth Di Collobiano, who was an accomplished amateur artist. She took the twins on art excursions, teaching them how to use watercolour and seeding the joy of painting in Fiona. 'Painting is a language,' she says. 'It's something that you can take with you anywhere. It keeps you company and feeds you, like playing the piano.'

At age ten, Fiona and Nencia relocated from their countryside idyll to Florence, where they started at a new school. Their informal art education also continued, much of it gleaned instinctively and very much centred on the language of colour. The earthy tones of limestone and terracotta of their rural home were replaced with the gently faded colours of their Florentine home, Palazzo Corsini al Prato. The magnificent grounds, seemingly brushed with every shade of green (flowers were used sparingly in classical Italian gardens), offered an alternative palette, ever-changing in the Tuscan light. The family's collection of beautifully preserved oil paintings, marking over 500 years of history, provided yet another selection of tones – rich and deeply saturated. The impact of these visual offerings on Fiona's artistic development has been profound and enduring.

After completing school, Fiona relocated to Brussels to train as a mural painter. In 1993, she married Riccardo Boatto in Venice and they went on to have three children, Leone, Neri and Zara. In 2001, eager to find an outlet for her creative impulses, she began working as a print designer in the Florentine studio of the late Emilio Pucci. Born the Marchese di Barsento, he was known in the fashion world as 'The Prince of Prints' and Fiona was drawn to his creative legacy. She worked at the company for five years, four of which were under Creative Director Christian Lacroix, who became an inspiring creative figure in her life: 'He took fashion to a different level. Beauty simply resonated with him – he would find it anywhere and everywhere.'

In 2004, after amicably divorcing Riccardo, Fiona married Diego di San Giuliano, grandson of Salvatore Ferragamo. Three more children, Fiamma, Fabiola and Lucio, were added to the brood. In testament to their collective warmth, generosity and maturity, Fiona, Riccardo and Diego are all close friends.

At age forty-six, Fiona decided to formalise her creative education with a three-year art degree at the Florence Academy of Art, a rigorous program with a strong focus on method and technique. It was only after eighteen months working exclusively in charcoal and pencil that the students were permitted to move on to oil paint.

— OPENING IMAGE
Fiona wanders through the walled *gardinetto* of the Marchesi di San Giuliano farm in Sicily, owned by her husband's family for over 800 years. Among tall palms and exotic specimens are bergamot trees and ornamental ponds with Star of Siam and Santa Cruz waterlilies.

— OPPOSITE
Fiona's studio, Florence.

— FOLLOWING FROM LEFT
— Leather-bound books of Fiona's watercolours that she gifted to her late father-in-law, the Marchese Giuseppe Paternò Castello di San Giuliano.

— The facade of the family's 15th-century home in Sicily.

These days, Fiona prefers to work in watercolour, and she often gifts her paintings to strangers in exchange for positive thoughts. The catalyst for this idea came in 2017, when a close friend became unwell. Fiona responded by dedicating several paintings to her and sharing them on Instagram along with warm and encouraging captions. Fiona's social media followers responded with further positive comments for her friend, creating a pool of good energy. The original painting, as well as a letter of gratitude, would then be sent to the person whose message resonated with Fiona the most. In the two years since she began the practice, hundreds of her works have been mailed around the globe. It's an entirely original approach in which Fiona has inadvertently circumvented the traditional gallery model to create a global following of collectors and supporters. These small acts of generosity seem somehow heroic in a time when art is so heavily commodified. With her paintings acting as a conduit, strangers feel connected in a meaningful way and a friend in need is offered dozens of uplifting messages from people around the world.

Fiona's artwork also infuses the walls of the home she shares with Diego and their children in Florence, a 16th-century estate located near the Boboli Gardens. Architect Themistocle Antoniadis was commissioned to help design the home by combining two of the property's ancient farm buildings and restoring their interiors. Fiona then worked in collaboration with British decorator Alexander Hamilton to bring the rooms alive with paint. Together with artist friends Francesca Guicciardini and Caterina Enni Misson, Fiona hand-stencilled a geometric Celtic motif in grey and soft-green on the walls of the master bedroom, a pattern that she had discovered in a book belonging to her grandmother. They painted frescoes on the drawing-room walls and installed Fiona's watercolour depictions of the Palazzo Corsini al Prato's garden as retro-illuminated panels in the dining room. By day they seem like gilded windows, but as the sun goes down the garden slowly emerges. 'The panels cover the walls of the room, so I feel like I have brought the garden into my house,' says Fiona. The interiors include an eclectic mix of furnishings and decor, from ancient tapestries, family heirlooms and precious artworks to flea market finds and handmade treasures.

'I really do believe that houses are portraits of those who create them,' Fiona says. Her spiritual connection with the natural world is reflected in her paintings, her homes and gardens and the flowers in her hair. She wears one of the red flowers in honour of her late father-in-law, who shared with her a deep connection to the Sicilian landscape and its produce. She wears the second red flower in memory of her adored nephew Filippo Corsini, who died in a cycling accident in London at age twenty-one. The third flower represents important female figures in Fiona's life, and she chooses a different woman to focus on each day. 'It might be for my grandmother or my mother-in-law. I started wearing them when my father-in-law died, and Nencia wears them too.'

For Fiona, flowers can also be teachers if we can just slow down for long enough to absorb their lessons. One gets the feeling that, like the blossoms in her garden, Fiona herself is in a constant state of metamorphosis, growing and evolving spiritually and creatively and bringing those she loves with her on a wonderful creative journey into a hopeful future.

† † †

— One of two cabinets in the master bedroom (also seen opposite) displaying a collection of Ferragamo shoes in Fiona and Diego's Florentine home. Diego's grandfather, Salvatore Ferragamo, founded the brand in Florence in 1927.

— **PREVIOUS LEFT
AND RIGHT**
Interiors from Palazzo
Corsini al Prato.

— **LEFT**
Detail from one of
Fiona's watercolours.

— **OPPOSITE**
The Renaissance-style garden
at Palazzo Corsini al Prato.
The garden is seen here in
its dormant winter state,
devoid of some 200 potted
citrus plants that have been
relocated to the large lemon
houses for protection during
the colder months.

— OPPOSITE AND ABOVE
Treasures from the Corsini
family archives, which are
carefully preserved in Villa Le
Corti in Chianti. Among the
papers are those of Lorenzo
Corsini, who became Pope
Clement XII in 1730.

— ABOVE AND OPPOSITE
Extensive archives
documenting the Corsini
family's cultural and political
achievements, dating back to
the 12th century, are preserved
in Villa Le Corti. Scholars can
apply for permission to conduct
research in the archives.

— **CLOCKWISE FROM TOP LEFT**

— Statue framed by Etruscan, Greek and Latin plaques under the loggia of Palazzo Corsini al Prato.

— Fiona's gilded charcoal study of a torso in her studio.

— A wall of succulents and cacti in the family home in Sicily.

— Watercolour studies taped to a board in Fiona's studio in Florence.

— Fiona walks through the ancient doors of a vast *limonaia*, or lemon house, on the grounds of the Palazzo Corsini al Prato.

— Garden scene at the Marchesi di San Giuliano farm in Sicily.

— Fiona's watercolour panels of the Palazzo Corsini al Prato's garden that line the dining room in her home in Florence.

95

· AUVERGNE, FRANCE ·

CLAIRE BASLER

· ARTIST ·

When Claire Basler was twelve, she had an epiphany in a Gothic palace in Avignon, France. While other youngsters might have been tugging at their parents' sleeves, begging for early release from sightseeing at the Palais des Papes, Claire was immovable inside its 14th-century walls. Enveloped on all sides by a panorama of ancient frescoes covering the walls of the late Pope Clement VI's private study, the Chambre du Cerf, she was overcome: 'I had the strong impression that I was not just *looking* at the painting, but was *part* of the painting.'

Claire's unique view of the world was inherited from her parents. Her father, French modernist architect Jean-Jacques Basler, and her mother, Bernadette Basler, refused to subscribe to the trends of their time. They avoided the crush of Parisian families heading to the coast for annual summer holidays in favour of mountain escapes to Jura, on the Swiss border. These trips had a profound impact on Claire, who shared her father's passion for nature: 'As a little girl growing up in Paris, I was very cloistered. We always had to be careful and be supervised. So, while it was not fashionable to go to Jura in August, for me, being in nature became synonymous with freedom – the calendula, the clover, the grass.'

Her father also ignored other trends. Growing up in a small village in rural France surrounded by fields and forests, he developed a passion for wildflowers. Claire remembers: 'When I was young it was very fashionable to have structured, stiff bouquets and yet he would make massive, exuberant floral creations.' He not only shared his interest in flowers with Claire but taught her how to really see them. The influence of his teachings on her artwork, her home's interiors and her outlook has been lifelong. 'We live in a very visually stimulating world, and yet we now spend less time actually *seeing* things,' she explains. 'You can spend your entire life thinking that everything is going wrong because you haven't been taught how to properly open your eyes. What is important about being able to really see is that it unlocks an innate sense of poetic vision, which is the basis of what it means to be artistic.'

For Claire, a simple flower has heightened meaning. Her use of flowers as subjects in both her paintings and interior installations at her home offers the viewer a new way of experiencing colour, structure, form and space. She believes the words 'decor' and 'decorative' have been abused, leading to a demise in the appreciation of flowers in themselves and as a subject in art. 'A flower is not simply an element of decor – it is alive,' she explains. 'Decor can be a fundamental expression of beauty, and beauty is intelligent – the motor of wisdom and understanding.'

Claire's floral paintings provide hope amid what can seem like insurmountable global problems. 'In the face of the world's violence, I express my pain and incomprehension with my hands,' she says. 'I turn to the complex beauty of flowers and I communicate with them in silence: crying, laughing or simply smiling in their wonderful company.' This spiritual closeness to and unspoken dialogue with nature provide Claire with a lifeline: 'If I couldn't be surrounded by nature, I would invent it through my artwork, or I would die.'

Claire was born in 1960 in the Parisian neighbourhood of Vincennes, located next to the largest public park in the city, the Bois de Vincennes, and she has remained close to nature ever since. For her, the natural world is not 'other' but 'self'. Without her symbiotic connection to the environment, she believes she could not produce art in the way she does: 'I recognise myself as much in the vitality of a tree as in its death, in the blooming of a flower as much as in its fading.' Her desire to enter into union with nature through her work drives her to the studio every day. There, she will often be found holding the subject of her painting in her left hand as she paints with a brush in her right.

— OPENING IMAGE
Service pantry leading through a corridor to a guest bedroom.

— OPPOSITE
The orangerie, which is sometimes used as an additional studio and exhibition space.

— FOLLOWING
The sitting room, which Claire has painted in a forest scene, where Claire and Pierre often host *aperitif* for local friends and visiting house guests before dinner.

— OPPOSITE
View through the entrance
gates towards the château's
main residential wing, with
a glimpse of the medieval
tower on the right.

Claire established her first painting studio in 1977, in a small attic space. Almost twenty years later, she set up her home and studio in a disused factory boiler room in Montreuil, Paris. It was there that she began observing flowers in new ways: 'Thanks to the zenithal light from a transparent roof, I learned more about the structure of flowers, the way they fit together and their logic.'

Since then, Claire has built a thriving art practice while also raising three children. Now based at Château de Beauvoir, located in the commune of Échassières in central France, Claire marries her life and work into one magnificent whole. She also found a great love and partner in Pierre Imhof, whom she met in 2006 in the small village of Les Ormes in Yonne.

When Claire and Pierre purchased Château de Beauvoir in 2011, it had no hot water, heating or electricity, but it did provide them with a joint project that would be ongoing for the foreseeable future. The property seemed perfect, with rare trees and ample space for areas of soft grass and clover. There was also a glasshouse and large additional buildings, including former stables, which would provide Claire with studios and exhibition spaces full of natural light. Pierre, a passionate builder with skills in welding, carpentry, masonry and electrical work, made plans to embark on a three-year restoration of the castle.

The reality of life in a castle initially proved brutal. In October 2011, soon after the couple moved in, the weather took a dramatic turn. With the temperature hovering between minus 10 and 20 °C, they were confined to two rooms and the studio was rendered unusable. The upside of being unable to work in her studio was that Claire felt compelled to start painting on the interior walls of the rooms they inhabited.

Now murals enliven almost every room, with nature the singular theme. Claire's belief in nature as healer, muse and protector is expressed in each work and in the interiors of the château. With her paintings as the backdrop, she installs bold floral arrangements, often using the same flowers as those depicted on the walls. Viewed in the half-light of early morning or in the dying light of a winter's dusk, the painted and the real become one.

Much like Claire at the Palais des Papes as a girl, house guests often feel they are inside her work. Traditional concepts of the viewer and the participant, and the blurring of lines between outdoors and in, transport visitors to a more wonderful world. Claire's dream of existing not *with* her paintings but *inside* them has been achieved, and she shares this dream with others.

† † †

— ABOVE
Claire at work in her studio.

— OPPOSITE
Firewood, flowers and forest
scenes form a rich visual
tapestry in the sitting room.

— FOLLOWING
Master bedroom with Claire's
dreamlike wall mural.

— ABOVE

A small sitting room in the château's guest wing, where fresh flowers meet their painted equivalents in a lyrical melding of colour and form.

— OPPOSITE

View past a linen curtain through the dining room.

108

— OPPOSITE
Corridor view through the
master bedroom.

— ABOVE
A greyscale visual symphony
in one of the château's many
guest bedrooms.

111

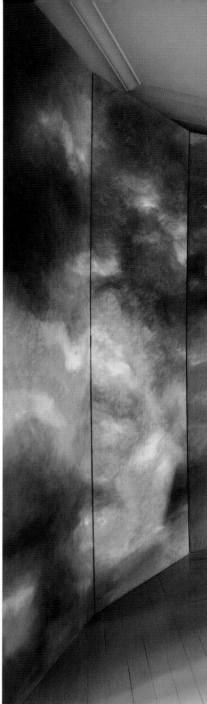

— OPPOSITE
One of Claire's murals covers
the walls and ceiling of the
dining room.

— ABOVE
Guest bedroom with Claire's
painted wall panels.

113

— CLOCKWISE FROM
BOTTOM LEFT

— Stone barn with white
wooden lattice doors.

— Paint pots in Claire's studio.

— Ancient staircase leading to
the guest wing.

— Pierre and Claire carry one
of her large canvases to the
studio, as their cat Cassandra
looks on.

— Cabinet inside the kitchen
pantry room.

— The main entrance gates to
the château.

— Pantry room with plates,
pots and a pumpkin sitting on
a stepladder.

— Daybeds in a sitting room in
the guest wing, surrounded by
Claire's cloud mural.

— External view of the orangerie.

· FLORENCE ·

SUE TOWNSEND

· CREATIVE
ENTREPRENEUR ·

For creative entrepreneur Sue Townsend, the Piazza del Duomo in Syracuse, on the isle of Ortigia, is the perfect Sicilian setting for her evening *aperitivo*. Architectural masterpieces adorn the square, but it is a family of Doric columns lining one side of the Duomo di Siracusa that most capture her imagination.

Originally part of a Greek temple built in the 5th century BCE to honour Athena, who was, among other things, the goddess of inspiration, wisdom and the arts, the pillars survived a catastrophic earthquake and tsunami in 1693 that destroyed much of the town; they were later integrated into the cathedral. It seems fitting that centuries after they were created for Athena, the elegant columns now inspire Sue, whose work combines inspiration, wisdom and the arts in equal measure.

Born in Britain, Sue is now a long-time resident of Italy, her love of the country ignited on family holidays there as a teenager. Florence captured her imagination with its elegant streetscapes and muted colour palette, but it was Sicily, with its crumbling historic interiors and architecture, that stole her heart. She was also fascinated by the multiple personalities of its terrain – the rocky bluffs and isolated villages contrasting with the tropical gardens and lush citrus groves that spring from fertile, magenta-coloured volcanic soil. She describes it as 'a fascinating mixture of the brutal and the beautiful'.

Her passion for gardens, though, was first awakened in childhood, on the family property in the Cotswolds. Her mother, Margaret Eileen Townsend, was an enthusiastic gardener whose delight in all things botanical was infectious. Her garden and the lush painterly vistas surrounding their home, coupled with the contrasting landscapes of Italy, provided Sue with important reference points for her later work.

Sue's reputation as a creative thinker and businesswoman was formed in the 1970s and 80s, after she helped establish Crabtree & Evelyn. The brand produced the most well known and loved English-garden-inspired home, bath and body products of its time. Along with botanical perfumes, scented creams, shower gels and bath salts, it also produced a range of premium food products, including tea, biscuits, marmalade and jam.

As Crabtree & Evelyn grew, Sue's interest subsided, and in 1990 she left. Soon after, Prince Charles invited her to join him as a director of Duchy Originals, where she helped create a selection of high-quality organic food products and establish a Duchy Originals store on the prince's Highgrove estate. But as the 20th century drew to a close, Sue decided it was time for a new adventure and she left her home in London for a new life in Florence. She now lives on the top floor of the 15th-century Palazzo Canigiani, located on the banks of the Arno, with views from her loggia to the Ponte Vecchio, the facade of the Basilica di Santa Croce and miles of terracotta rooftops.

From her base in Florence, Sue is a frequent visitor to Sicily, where, when not in Ortigia, she often stays as a guest at the San Giuliano farm. A 15th-century villa set in a magical nearly 9-hectare estate, it is located between Catania and Syracuse, in an area known as Sicilia Orientale due to its tropical climate and proximity to Africa. Marchese Giuseppe Paternò Castello di San Giuliano and his wife, shoe designer Fiamma Ferragamo (scion of Italy's famous Ferragamo footwear family), lovingly created the garden over a period of twenty-five years. The property was later inherited by their son Diego di San Giuliano, who visits regularly with his wife, artist Fiona Corsini, and their six children.

The garden's diverse vegetation and intoxicating colours and scents enthralled Sue from her first visit to the farm: 'There are exotic plants, a huge Moreton Bay fig tree, fragrant jasmine and patches of cacti, and the orange groves go on for miles. And what's more remarkable is that all these different plants grow next to each other with a view of Mount Etna.'

— OPENING IMAGE
An embroidered Turkish robe hangs from a lacquered Queen Anne cabinet in the master bedroom.

— OPPOSITE
The 15th-century internal courtyard in the building adjoining Palazzo Canigiani is attributed to master Renaissance architect Michelozzo di Bartolomeo Michelozzi, a favourite of Cosimo de' Medici.

VII

It was among the fragrant trees, citrus plantations and rare specimens of the expansive park that the concept for Sue's next creative venture began to take shape. She was so enamoured with their perfumes that she dreamed of bottling them to share with others. In effect, that is what she did, creating a line of pure, organic bath, body and home products based on the botanical extracts and essences of Sicily. To help her with the project, Italy's most famous perfumer, Lorenzo Villoresi, was commissioned to distil the distinctly Sicilian scents of the flowers and plants.

Sue wanted to create a name for the brand that encapsulated the best of Sicily: its natural beauty, art, architecture and history. One evening, while sitting in her usual spot in 'the perfect Sicilian setting', the Piazza del Duomo in Ortigia, it suddenly became obvious and 'Ortigia Sicilia' was officially launched in 2006.

Sue draws from Sicily's ancient culture and history to develop the brand's visual identity, from the logo and packaging to the store decor and products. When she discovers a centuries-old print or motif that captures her imagination, she adapts it for use in her designs. One such image was inspired by the 12th-century Sassanian Persian mosaics in Palermo's Palazzo dei Normanni. In recent years, Sue has expanded her range to include Sicilian-inspired velvet, linen and leather totes, handbags and wallets. There are silk and cashmere scarves, caftans, cotton beach dresses and artisan-crafted enamel jewellery. Sue donates a percentage of Ortigia profits to charities that rescue, care for and work to rehouse abandoned dogs in Italy and Africa.

Despite her British heritage, Sue runs Ortigia like an Italian matriarch might run her family — with warmth, wisdom, energy and directness, and a great eye for detail. She gains as much satisfaction from nurturing and encouraging her employees as she does from the creative aspects of her work. 'Ortigia has a family atmosphere,' she explains, 'and my aim is to make things I believe in.' At every stage, she has remained true to her initial vision — celebrating the unique offerings of Sicilian gardens — by creating products she loves using herself.

Having visited the San Giuliano garden that first inspired Sue, as well as the piazza in Ortigia where she came up with the brand's name, I can confirm that if you breathe in the scent of the soaps, shower gels and salts, you will be transported for a moment into another, more beautiful world.

† † †

— **PREVIOUS FROM LEFT**
— **An 18th-century Dutch mirror in the sitting room.**

— **A four-poster Regency Chinese bed in the master bedroom.**

— **OPPOSITE**
A sumptuous mix of antiques contrasts with the vivid magenta silk–covered armchair.

— **FOLLOWING**
The circular dining room with hand-blocked linen wallcoverings.

— A reading corner in
Sue's library framed by a
large bookcase.

— OPPOSITE
Sitting room with plush sofas
and armchairs, dozens of silk
and velvet cushions and a
19th-century Indian floor rug.

— FOLLOWING
A 19th-century statue of the
Roman goddess Venus in the
entrance hall. Panel designs
on the walls (seen above the
doorway) mirror those of the
apartment's front door, seen in
the image on the right.

— CLOCKWISE FROM
BOTTOM LEFT

— The grand bluestone
staircase that leads to
Sue's apartment.

— Marble bust of Apollo in
the loggia.

— Ortigia, Sicily, the place
that inspired the name of
Sue's company.

— Cushion detail in the
sitting room.

— Master bedroom detail with
18th-century rococo mirror.

— Sitting room with a mix
of British and European
antiques and artworks.

— Sue in the loggia with
views of Florence.

· NEW YORK ·
· VIRGINIA ·

BEATRIX OST

· PHILOSOPHER ·
· ARTIST ·

O<!-- drop cap -->n the banks of the Hudson River in Upstate New York, in the historic village of Cold Spring, Beatrix Ost's newly renovated house was on fire. The 1981 blaze wiped out a year's worth of repairs and restorations and destroyed the plans she had for her new family home and art studio. It also claimed a lifetime of personal treasures, including hundreds of artworks. It took months for Beatrix to recover from the trauma and loss.

With her dream of a property in Upstate New York extinguished, it was time to begin the search for a new home. Consulting her pendulum, a tool used to seek spiritual and material guidance, Beatrix and her husband, Ludwig Kuttner, settled upon Virginia. There, among the undulating landscapes of southern Albemarle County, she found a farm with echoes of her Bavarian childhood. Set on a hill, surrounded by a 200-hectare estate, was a two-storey Roman Revival home, Estouteville.

The historically significant property was designed in the style of Thomas Jefferson's iconic mansion, Monticello, by his master carpenter, James Dinsmore. He began building Estouteville in 1827 and integrated several Jeffersonian design features into the plans. Doric entablature and white trims, red bricks made in a Williamsburg factory and tetrastyle Tuscan order porticoes on the front and rear facades all contributed to the stately appearance.

Before long, Beatrix began hosting a salon on the first Monday of each month. News of the home's sculpture-filled garden and eclectic interiors travelled quickly among artistically minded locals and over the years her salon events grew to epic proportions, with up to 200 people in attendance. Guests were as enthralled by the house as by their hostess's infectious sense of fun and wide-ranging conversations. In one parlour, an antique silk damask sofa was arranged as though in conversation with a pair of Texan-style cattle-horn armchairs. In the same room, a gilded ancestral portrait and a collection of Beatrix's figurative paintings were placed near a row of her wax sculptures of human and animal heads. Across the hall in a second sitting room, a collection of German *Jugendstil* pewterware featured on large shelves, while Art Nouveau lamps and light fittings adorned side tables, consoles and mantels throughout the house.

Beatrix was born near Stuttgart, Germany, in 1940, and her experience growing up during World War II and its aftermath helped define her adult life. Her formative years were lived at Goldachof, a large working farm 30 kilometres north of Munich. The relative safety of the property's location meant that friends, close and distant relatives and strangers sought refuge there during and after the war. As her parents were often busy looking after their many house guests, Beatrix used her imagination and creativity to entertain herself, igniting a lifelong passion for art and literature. Though both parents were active in assisting those affected by the war, their differing approaches – her mother was hopeful, her father a pessimist – offered Beatrix a powerful early lesson that was reinforced in her adult life when she studied Tibetan Buddhism: 'You can train your body and mind to be positive – we are human and we have negative thoughts, but you can choose to focus on the beautiful and eventually the negatives will float away.'

In 1953, at age thirteen, Beatrix was sent to boarding school in Munich. After finishing high school, she began studying painting at the Academy of Fine Arts in Munich. Each summer, she attended the 'School of Seeing' in Salzburg under the tutelage of its founder, expressionist artist Oskar Kokoschka. Enthralled by 'the art of vision', Kokoschka offered an immersive program encompassing the creative, technical, political, philosophical and social. It was a holistic art education, which Beatrix embraced and which provided her

with a creative platform that infused every aspect of her later life. Building on Kokoschka's teachings, she established a practice where no art form or artistic medium was off limits. She threw herself into the visual and performing arts, making a living from portrait commissions, acting and modelling.

At age twenty, she married a charming and free-spirited archaeologist, writer and wanderer called Ferdinand. In the early years of the marriage their apartment was a revolving door of bohemian hedonism, their relationship bound together by 'a sort of complicity against the boredom of the conformist life' around them. After having two children together, however, Beatrix's life with Ferdinand began to unravel and they separated.

Thereafter, freed from the challenges of the relationship, she continued to build a life in Munich, with her two sons, as a successful artist, actor and model. In September 1968 she met Ludwig Kuttner, a dashing and kind man with an eye for style, and they dated for three years before moving in together. Their son, Fabian, was born in 1974, and a year later, ready for a new adventure, the family emigrated to the United States, settling in New York.

In June 1975, the city's crime and drug problems had many residents leaving in droves. As a result, real estate was cheap and artists swarmed in to live in sprawling lofts and revel in the city's underbelly. 'As New York neared bankruptcy and people fled to suburbia, we bought a penthouse on 67th Street between Park and Lex for $175,000,' Beatrix recalls. A short walk from Central Park, the Upper East Side apartment had six bedrooms, four bathrooms, formal entertaining areas, maids' quarters and expansive terraces.

By November 1981, the Upper East Side was one of the more gentrified areas of the city, a world away from the dangerous streets of downtown. For Beatrix, life itself became a work of art, encompassing her painting, sculpture, clothes, jewellery and home, as well as her outlook, social events and relationships. Attending a dinner party at her penthouse was akin to being part of a performance piece, with guests dressing to a set theme. Beatrix might ask them to come decked out entirely in black and would serve food and beverages in a single colour only, such as red.

Never one to follow trends, Beatrix has always dressed for her own amusement, living by the adage: 'Dress for yourself so you feel good about the day.' For Beatrix, this means dyeing her hair a soft shade of blue (using vegan and cruelty-free colour) or choosing magnificent outfits to wear while wandering through Central Park. On the farm, she'll be seen striding across the lawn in a hand-painted silk skirt, a top of her own design, fishnet stockings and custom-made lace-up ankle boots. Four rings always adorn her fingers: she designed two of them based on tree branches from the property and the others were purchased by Ludwig at Codognato, in Venice, as gifts.

Unsurprisingly, Beatrix's artistic and philosophical outlook attracts like-minded women to her circle. Nigerian-American architect and thought-leader Oshoke Pamela Abalu (pictured on page 142) is one of her closest friends. They share a passion for ideas and Mother Earth, and the belief that love can change the world. They also both choose to wear evening gowns during the day and allow their hearts to lead them to new adventures.

To balance life in the heart of New York City, Beatrix actively creates time for periods of silence and contemplation. When she needs quiet, she wears a brooch she designed that reads 'practising silence'. If someone at a party tries to talk to her when she's wearing it, she points to the brooch and smiles, and suddenly the dynamic shifts. The ritual allows her to approach talking and listening, sound and silence, in a considered way, trading city-life cacophony for connection to her deeper self.

Over her lifetime, Beatrix's belief in self-efficacy has remained a constant: 'I know that through life, happiness is within yourself. It's like a fruit or a flower that you carry wherever you go.' Perhaps now, with all she has experienced, she also carries an inner pendulum that guides every decision and ensures she lives each day to the full.

† † †

— PREVIOUS
Beatrix holds one of her beeswax sculptures in the sitting room of her New York duplex apartment, located inside the Hotel des Artistes on West 67th Street.

— OPPOSITE
Estouteville's sitting room features a diverse mix of 19th- and 20th-century artworks and objects along with works by Beatrix and her friends. The large painting is Beatrix's own, titled *Boy with a Snake, Girl with a Bird*, 1985.

— PREVIOUS
The New York City apartment's sitting room, with a floor rug and daybeds of Beatrix's design. The tiles on the fireplace read: 'Life is always being interrupted by events.'

— OPPOSITE
Beatrix (right) with one of her closest friends, Oshoke Pamela Abalu, who is the co-founder of Love & Magic Company, which designs workspaces based on thoughtfulness, energy flow and inclusivity.

— ABOVE
A reading corner inside Beatrix's apartment in Charlottesville, Virginia, the city local to the Estouteville property.

— CLOCKWISE FROM
BOTTOM LEFT

— View from the front verandah at Estouteville, with spherical marble sculpture *El Mundo*, 1990, by Beatrix Ost.

— Carved-wood Empire chair upholstered in yellow velvet on the upper floor of the New York City duplex. The unsigned portraits were inherited from a friend.

— Guest bedroom in Beatrix's New York apartment, with striped wallcoverings and floral-patterned furniture.

— Estouteville's front facade.

— Beatrix is a passionate collector of furniture, art, design and ephemera, including these hand motifs made from paper, metal and porcelain.

— The master bedroom of the apartment in Charlottesville, with a portrait of Beatrix's grandmother as a child that was painted by her father, Theodore Roeghels, in 1870.

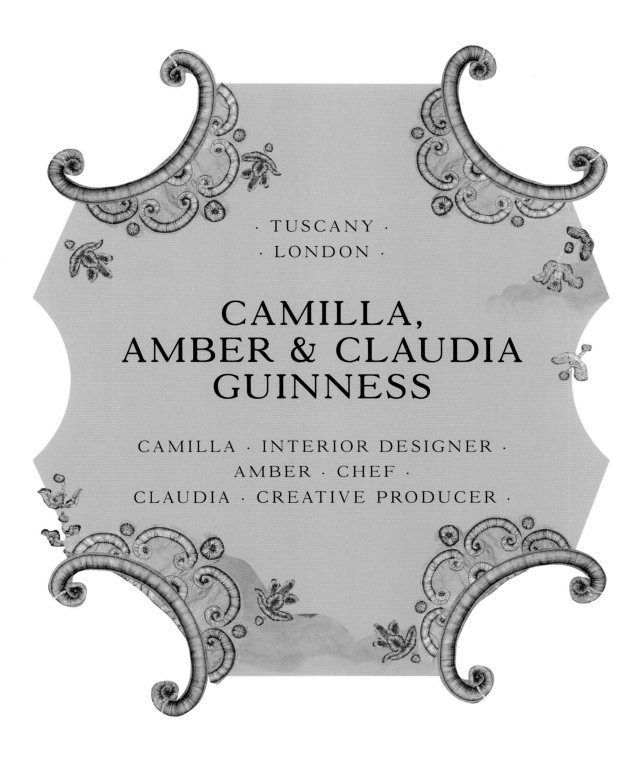

· TUSCANY ·
· LONDON ·

CAMILLA, AMBER & CLAUDIA GUINNESS

CAMILLA · INTERIOR DESIGNER ·
AMBER · CHEF ·
CLAUDIA · CREATIVE PRODUCER ·

When visiting her godfather's 17th-century Tuscan home, Villa Cetinale, as a child, Amber Guinness would run barefoot for hours on the manicured grass with her younger sister, Claudia. They would dart around cypress trees and topiary bushes shaped into balls and cones until called to the table for lunch. Their parents, Jasper and Camilla Guinness, could often be found in the sun by the back terrace with the villa's owner, Antony 'Tony' Lambton (the 6th Earl of Durham), and his companion Claire Ward.

Tony and his family were also frequent visitors at the Guinnesses' home, Arniano, located just over half an hour's drive south. The two properties have much in common, though architecture is not one of them. Cetinale was built in 1680 in the Roman Baroque style, while Arniano, a traditional stone-and-brick Tuscan farmhouse, dates from the 18th century. What they share is much-loved gardens. Tony was passionate about Cetinale's magnificent grounds and Jasper, a botanist and self-taught landscape designer, was never happier than when working on Arniano's garden, which was a continual work in progress. Another common feature of both properties is interiors designed by Camilla.

Camilla's feeling for fabric, colour, texture and form were developed during her childhood in England, in the workshop of her mother, artist and fashion designer Sally Uniacke. During the 1960s Sally created clothes for her small label, Cat Designs. As a child, Camilla witnessed the industrious machinations of her mother's creative world, from concept drawings, fabric choices and pattern making to watching seamstresses give form to the designs.

From the outset, Camilla applied what she learned not to designing clothes but to creating interiors. And the barns of the family's rural home near England's south coast provided her with plenty of opportunities. Her interiors projects served to answer both a creative and an emotional need: 'I couldn't bear to be in a place that I didn't like the look of,' she says. 'It would affect my mood and make me unhappy.'

In 1968, when Camilla was nine years old, her mother died in a car accident. It was a terrible shock. 'I feel there were "before" and "after" periods,' Camilla explains. 'I wanted to be like her in some ways, but for many years after her death I was very shut down.' With few avenues available for her to process the loss, it was not surprising that things began to unravel at school; at age sixteen, after countless warnings, she was expelled. During a subsequent stint at finishing school, she learned to cook, then used those skills to work and travel through Europe and the United States before enrolling in a furniture restoration course in Florence.

Meanwhile, after completing a law degree at Oxford, Camilla's future husband, Jasper Guinness, had also left England on his way to sunnier shores. The son of Irish brewing heir Jonathan Guinness (3rd Baron Moyne) and his first wife, Ingrid, he was drawn to Europe perhaps as much as he was repelled from Britain by the parental and societal expectations that risked suffocating him.

Jasper and Camilla met in Florence, and after marrying in 1985 they based themselves in Chianti before purchasing Arniano, a run-down farmhouse near Montalcino. While the home was in poor condition and lacked basic utilities, it was surprisingly spacious, with high ceilings and generously sized rooms. And beyond the barren grounds were magnificent views of Tuscany.

Jasper and Camilla set up camp with baby Amber and got to work transforming Arniano with the help of local contractors. Camilla focused on the interiors and Jasper took responsibility for the garden. Indoors, a wall on the ground floor was demolished to make

— PREVIOUS
Amber preparing lunch for
friends in Arniano's kitchen.

— OPPOSITE
Arniano's main entrance area,
with soft shapes mirroring the
surrounding landscape.

way for a large main living area. Fireplaces and utilities were built in, a series of wide shelves, a large stove and a waist-high wood-fired oven were installed in the kitchen and ancient stone and tile floors were repaired throughout. Camilla also designed four-poster bedframes for many of the bedrooms, salvaging a linen-trimmed crown canopy from an abandoned house to mount above the bed in one.

By the time Claudia was born in 1992, a stream of house guests had begun arriving. Camilla would hold forth in the kitchen, preparing regional specialities from seasonal ingredients, while Jasper served drinks in the garden – or by the fire on cooler evenings – until the meal was served. Eventually, Amber and Claudia began helping their mother in the kitchen, preparing impromptu weekend lunches for fifteen or more and summer dinners for up to forty.

When Amber and Claudia were almost of high school age, it became clear that while they'd received an excellent Italian education at the local school, their English studies had suffered. In 2003 the family relocated to England. The decade that followed was, for them, one of enormous change and challenge.

Amber's godfather, Tony Lambton, died in 2006. His son, Edward 'Ned' Lambton, succeeded him as the 7th Earl of Durham and inherited Villa Cetinale. Camilla was subsequently asked to help refresh the interiors. While working on the project, Jasper became ill and died of cancer in May 2011, at fifty-seven years of age. The loss was felt profoundly not only by Camilla, Amber and Claudia but also by his extended family and many friends.

In the aftermath of her father's death, Amber looked for a way to reconnect with the home and country of her childhood. Since relocating to the United Kingdom, she had visited Arniano infrequently and missed her father's beloved garden, the gentle Tuscan views, the regional culture and the cuisine. Coincidentally, her best friend, artist William Roper-Curzon, was looking for a continental adventure and they came up with the idea of hosting a painting retreat for small groups. William would teach art classes, while Amber would produce inspiring regional dishes for the guests. Thus, the Arniano Painting School was established in 2014.

In reconnecting with her childhood home, Amber has injected Arniano with new life and affirmed her love of Tuscany. Unsurprisingly, when she and journalist Matthew Bell married in 2016, they decided to live in Italy. They divide their time between Florence and Arniano, with regular visits to Wiltshire, in England.

Claudia, who works as an assistant creative producer in London, has also found a way to balance life in England with time at Arniano, which she tries to visit every year. Like her mother and sister, she has developed a strong creative side, which she channels into photography. After purchasing a vintage camera in 2017, she now regularly buys film, often black and white, and sticks the prints into a large album. 'I love looking through my parents' photo albums and I love the idea of creating them for my own future family. I can almost imagine my child looking at them and thinking, "Oh, look. There's Aunt Amber when she was living in Florence".'

The positive impacts of her childhood in Arniano continue to resonate with Claudia. 'Growing up in Italy was slow-paced…we would be taken on four-hour lunches. It does mean that it is hard to get anything done, but as a child it was so nice because I got to spend so much time with my parents and friends – it was so much more relaxed.'

Amber's painting school guests have produced hundreds of artworks immortalising Arniano's magic, the results of which are displayed in the homes of their creators around the world, like colourful reminders to live well. Even without a Tuscan villa, many of the main ingredients can be adopted by others: nurturing meals, creativity, convivial interiors and a close relationship with nature. Added to this are love and friendship, which the Guinnesses have in spades and happily share with their many guests.

† † †

— OPPOSITE
One of Arniano's bedrooms,
with a wall mural by artist
Virginia Loughnan and a bed
designed by Camilla.

— ABOVE
Camilla (seated) and Amber
Guinness at Arniano.

— **ABOVE**
Villa Cetinale, the interiors of
which Camilla helped decorate
and restore.

— **OPPOSITE**
An arch in the Arniano sitting
room leads to a guest bedroom
on the ground floor.

— **FOLLOWING FROM LEFT**
— Detail of an antique
baldachin bed on the *piano
nobile* at Villa Cetinale.

— When Villa Cetinale's
owners, Ned and Marina
Lambton, asked Camilla to
help with the interiors, the aim
was to 'keep things feeling the
same, but a comfortable version
of what had been'.

160

— CLOCKWISE FROM
BOTTOM LEFT

— Garden detail, Arniano.

— Detail of upholstered
chair and ceramic pot with
olive branches in the Arniano
sitting room.

— View from the Arniano
garden to the olive groves.

— Sitting room detail, Arniano.

— One of the guest bedrooms
at Villa Cetinale.

— *Cypresses and Olive Tree at
Arniano*, 2019, by Amber's best
friend, William Roper-Curzon.

— William Roper-Curzon
paints in the garden at Arniano.

— Entrance hall, Arniano.

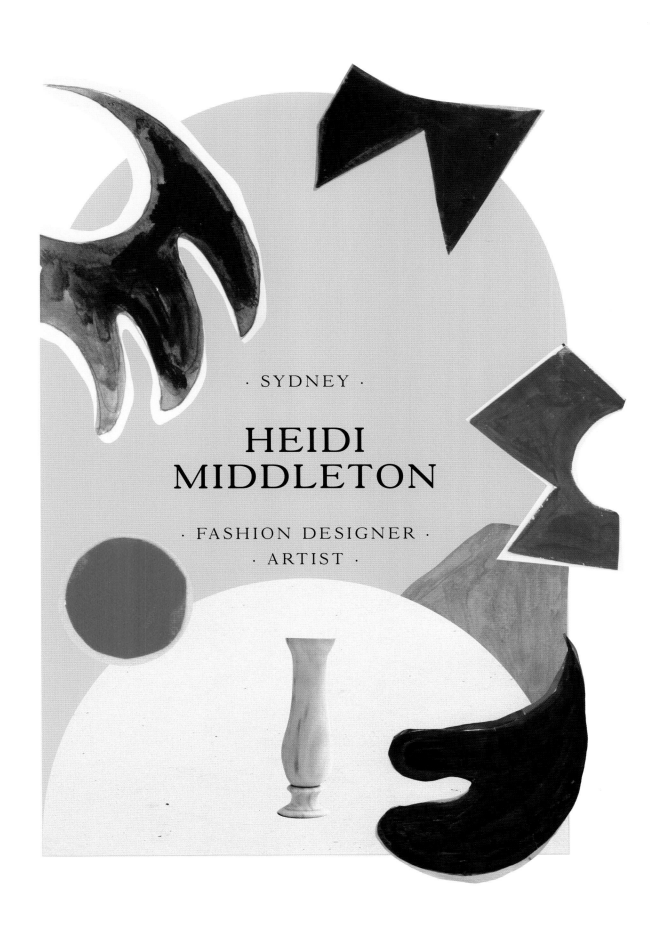

· SYDNEY ·

HEIDI MIDDLETON

· FASHION DESIGNER ·
· ARTIST ·

T

The urban fringes of Queensland towns and cities in the early 1970s did not produce many fashion designers. Instead, the largely subtropical climate of Australia's third most populous state tended to give rise to farmers and surfers, homemakers and small business owners.

Internationally acclaimed Australian fashion designer Heidi Middleton was only three years old when she moved with her parents and elder brother to the rural outskirts of Queensland's capital city, Brisbane. Until that point, the family had lived in the conservative enclave of Sydney's North Shore. 'My parents are both quite free-spirited, and I think they felt a bit claustrophobic in the city and needed to break free and go on an adventure.'

After studying Commercial Art at Queensland College of Art, then working in advertising as an art director, Heidi joined forces with a local friend, Sarah-Jane Clarke, and started making clothes. They set their sights on a global platform. The first stop was London, where they sold jeans at the Portobello Market. Then in 1999, when their visas were due to expire, they returned to Australia and launched what was to become a cult label: Sass & Bide. Within ten years it had become an international fashion empire.

When Heidi met her future husband in 2003, the business was in full flight. He proposed after a twelve-week courtship and together they began house-hunting, focusing their attention on the Palm Beach peninsula of Sydney's Northern Beaches. The sunny 1940s home they found provided Heidi with a vital counterpoint to the increasing demands of the business, which felt 'like a friendly, hungry monster that needed constant feeding'. With three fashion lines under the one label and up to four ranges presented each year, long holidays were rare. Heidi and Sarah-Jane covered for each other when their children were born, but in 2007, when Heidi took time off for the birth of her second daughter, Elke, she was forced on an extended break when, twelve hours after the birth, she was diagnosed with breast cancer. After treatment, she made a full recovery.

By 2011, Heidi and Sarah-Jane were ready for a change. They sold the controlling share of their company and stayed on as creative consultants until the remaining share of the business was sold in 2014, and then stepped out of it altogether. Now free to travel, Heidi and her family moved to France for a twelve-month sabbatical. They settled into a light-filled Parisian apartment in the eighth arrondissement and Heidi found a studio in the north-western neighbourhood of Clignancourt, where she reignited her love of painting, drawing, collage and ceramics.

During a weekend in the Médoc region of south-western France visiting their friends Mimi and Oddur Thorrison, Heidi and her husband went house-hunting. Mimi was a great ambassador for the area and 'really sold the region to us', recalls Heidi. 'It's wild and rugged, but there is a poetry and romance to the landscape and the old villages.' They went to see an 1830s manor house, Les Tourelles, in Saint-Christoly-Médoc that Mimi had described as 'a rough diamond'. The five-bedroom home was set on 3 hectares and included an orchard, a small vineyard, a dairy and a barn. Despite having been uninhabited for several years and feeling somewhat derelict, its foundations were strong and it had elegant proportions, with turrets framing the facade and interiors with 4-metre ceilings. For Heidi, the potential for transformation was intoxicating. They made an offer and three days later owned the home. 'The idea was for my husband to host meditation retreats in Bordeaux and for me to start a new fashion and art business called ArtClub,' says Heidi. 'This was going to be chapter two of living in France.'

Before a full renovation could begin, the entire home needed to be gutted. With Mimi's list of trusted local tradesmen on the job, Heidi and her family left for a summer break in Australia. On their way back to France, her husband peeled off to go to India for ten

— OPENING IMAGE
Heidi at home in Palm Beach.

— OPPOSITE
ArtClub designs in progress in the studio.

days. They were to meet again in Bordeaux to begin renovating their new home in earnest. When they reunited, however, they acknowledged that there had been a tangible shift in the relationship and made the decision to separate. After her husband left France, Heidi began renovating the house and the girls started at the school in the local village.

While rebuilding their home's interiors, Heidi also began reimagining her vision for the future. Mother Nature provided welcome moments of pure joy. 'I was so inspired and stimulated by nature. I was constantly stopping the car and thinking how beautiful it all was. It helped carry me through,' she explains.

After a year of renovating and a second year filling the new home with friends, family, love and creativity, the future looked bright: 'I remember thinking I needed to surround myself with great people, good food and flowers. I decided that every mealtime I'd light candles, have music playing and cook for the girls.' Heidi began to view her experiences through a new lens. 'By the time we left France in 2018, I was happy and the house was finished. I wouldn't change what happened – there had been so much growth and self-reflection.'

Back in Sydney, her lovingly incubated creative concept, ArtClub, was born. The online-only atelier offers rare vintage garments for sale along with Heidi's paintings and original clothing designs. The antithesis of fast fashion, each new piece is created from remnant fabric that she saves from landfill, and is designed to be handed down through generations. They are sewn in Heidi's atelier by local collaborators, each of whom signs and numbers the garments like limited-edition artworks before they are mailed to customers.

Heidi initially set up ArtClub in a warehouse space in the city's south, but with the commute home to the north of Sydney equating to time away from her girls, it didn't feel right. She gave herself permission to make a change and moved ArtClub into her home in the suburb of Mosman. The move brought a new buzz and energy to the company, and Heidi continues to adjust her life to find the right rhythm and flow.

Heidi has created a loving local and international community. She keeps her precious daughters close, together with family members, her small team at ArtClub and a loyal network of creative women friends. In continuing to live with an open heart and express her inner world through art, fashion, poetry and interiors, she has become an inspiring example to like-minded women around the world.

† † †

— OPPOSITE
The master bedroom in
Palm Beach has views across
Pittwater and Sydney's
Northern Beaches.

— ABOVE
The bath in the master
bedroom, Palm Beach.

— CLOCKWISE FROM
TOP LEFT

— Garden view, Palm Beach.

— Atelier detail.

— Archway leading to the Palm Beach garden.

— Geometric shapes mixed with soft curves inform Heidi's paintings, the design of many of her ArtClub pieces and the interiors of her homes.

— A family of potted plants on the lower terrace at Palm Beach.

— Heidi with one of her best friends, photographic artist Jo Yeldham, who lives locally.

— Palm Beach living room.

· SICILY ·

· MILAN ·

LUCILLA BONACCORSI BECCARIA & LUISA BECCARIA

· FASHION DESIGNERS ·

Fashion designer Lucilla Bonaccorsi Beccaria seems as carefree and down-to-earth as a *signorina* from a small Italian village, though her heritage is loaded with the sort of unspoken expectation that might weigh heavily on the shoulders of someone less confident. Her father, Don Lucio Bonaccorsi dei Principi di Reburdone, is a Sicilian prince. Her mother, Luisa Beccaria, is a celebrated international fashion designer from a northern Italian family of intellectuals and prominent cultural figures.

As a teenager, Luisa couldn't find clothes that reflected her unique taste or fit her lithe frame properly, so she began making her own. Soon, she was creating highly feminine neo-Romantic dresses and gowns, which few designers were doing at the time. In doing so she established a new genre that was later to become fashionable around the world.

Historical references and the private world of old Milan infiltrated Luisa's work from the outset. One of her earliest collections was made using reclaimed Italian crocheted pieces and old curtains, which she cut, dyed and repurposed into gowns, jackets and pants. Her first parades took place not on the catwalk during Fashion Week but in the hidden courtyards, cobbled laneways and ancient convents of Milan's historic centre. She also exhibited her dresses like artworks, alongside designer and artist Piero Fornasetti's unique pieces in his influential Milan gallery in 1979 and 1980.

In 1981, Luisa met Lucio at one of her fashion shows. They married two years later, when Luisa was twenty-three, and the following year, Lucilla, their 'little light', came into the world. Four more children followed: Lucrezia, Ludovico, Luna and Luchino. Far from slowing down, Luisa wove her family and work life together in one big, happy tangle.

In 1984, the same year Lucilla was born, Luisa opened her flagship store, which was followed later by a second store dedicated to children's clothes. Lucilla grew up in the heart of her mother's business. As a child, she spent her after-school hours in Luisa's home office or in her atelier in Milan's Brera neighbourhood, making things from fabric, ribbons and silk-covered buttons. Inspired by her mother, Lucilla soon attempted her first designs, spurred by her upcoming Holy Communion. Inspiration for her outfit was found in a film trilogy based on the life of Princess Sisi of Austria. She made a number of sketches before a tailor was called in to take measurements. Luisa oversaw proceedings, and after several fittings, Lucilla appeared in her own designs – a lace dress and matching jacket – for the first time.

Lucilla witnessed her mother's trajectory from being one of Italy's most beloved designers to recognition on a global scale. Her poetic gowns and dresses were soon stocked in stores from Bergdorf Goodman in New York to Harrods in London, and being worn by royalty and celebrities from the Middle East to Hollywood.

As she grew older, Lucilla's love of design continued to develop and over time she became her mother's muse and a natural brand ambassador. By 2006, when Lucilla was at university, she was collaborating with her mother in the design department and slowly gaining experience and expertise. In 2014, she was officially appointed co-designer, with the responsibility of creating the prêt-à-porter collections. She also began designing jewellery, headpieces, shoes and bags, and today robust dialogue between mother and daughter feeds the creative cauldron of ideas in the atelier. Recently, the business has become a lifestyle brand with a home- and tableware line, including pink cut-glass champagne flutes, porcelain plates and fine linen table napkins embroidered with tiny flowers.

When they are not working, the family can often be found in their home in Milan, convening over lunch or dinner. Mealtimes are sacred for Luisa, representing a regular and important opportunity to bring everyone together. Even in the busiest times, she eats with

— OPENING IMAGE
Lucilla and Luisa in the family home in Milan.

— OPPOSITE
Ethereal gowns and dresses in the Luisa Beccaria boutique in Milan.

— PREVIOUS
Lucilla and husband Filippo
Richeri Vivaldi Pasqua's
apartment in Milan.

— OPPOSITE
Lucilla in the sitting room of
the family home in Milan.

— FOLLOWING
Informal dining room in
Castelluccio, Sicily.

her family as often as possible. And when they're not at home in Milan, they might well be at Castelluccio, the family's baroque castle in Sicily, eating outdoors, seated among the olive trees or at a long candlelit table under the jacarandas. With produce harvested from the kitchen garden and surrounding farmland, and traditional unleavened bread baked in a woodfired oven, it's easy to see why Lucilla and her siblings inherited their parents' passion for food.

Luisa was responsible for convincing Lucio that they should restore Castelluccio after it had been unoccupied for eight decades. As she explains, 'I fell in love with the place when it was in total decay. I was drawn to the romance, poetry and remoteness of it all. I loved its blond stone, its strong soul.'

They began by renovating four rooms on the ground floor, to give the family somewhere to eat and sleep while the almonds were being harvested. Luisa was determined not to overpower the castle's original pared-back beauty: 'We were actually very fortunate that the property had been sleeping for over seventy years, as its simple essence had not been destroyed.' For Lucilla, who was ten when they began the renovation, Castelluccio became an essential thread in the fabric of her life – so much so that she chose it as the location of her 2017 wedding to Filippo Richeri Vivaldi Pasqua.

Lucilla's siblings have also been influenced and inspired by their parents' work and their love of Sicily. Lucio oversees the family's thriving agribusiness, and in 2013 Lucilla, Lucrezia and Ludovico combined forces to create a series of 1950s-inspired food trucks in Sicily under an umbrella business name: LùBar. Their dream was to serve 'slow street food' Sicilian-style, with homemade arancini, almond milk, cocktails and cannoli. After the overwhelming success of their foray into the business of food, they imported the idea to Milan and in 2017 opened the first LùBar bistro at Villa Reale. Lucrezia designed the interiors for the cafe and Ludovico took on the role of operations manager. Lucilla dives in when required to offer creative advice and guidance.

Given that home is such a creative focal point for the family in both Milan and Sicily, it is not surprising that the Luisa Beccaria brand has expanded to encompass an entire universe of style. From authentic Sicilian food, interiors and tableware to gowns for royal balls and beach-ready caftans, it provides a blueprint for romantics the world over. Armed with their impressive cultural heritage, Lucilla and her siblings are continuing the traditions established by their parents in the most modern of ways.

† † †

Quod - Superest

Cotto per Micci   Thè Zafarana   Oggetti di

Maccheroni di
Napoli

...rina Maiorca — Ceci-Sapone

...mola   ed al...

Pasta di Casa

Vermicelli di
Napoli

— CLOCKWISE FROM
BOTTOM LEFT

— Castelluccio garden.

— From left: Luna, Lucilla,
Luisa and Lucrezia on the
terrace at the family home
in Milan, all wearing Luisa
Beccaria designs.

— Lucilla reflected in a
floor-to-ceiling mirror.

— Dresses on display at the
Luisa Beccaria boutique
in Milan.

— View from the terrace
at Castelluccio.

— Entrance area at LùBar on
Villa Reale in Milan.

— Views of the farmland
surrounding Castelluccio.

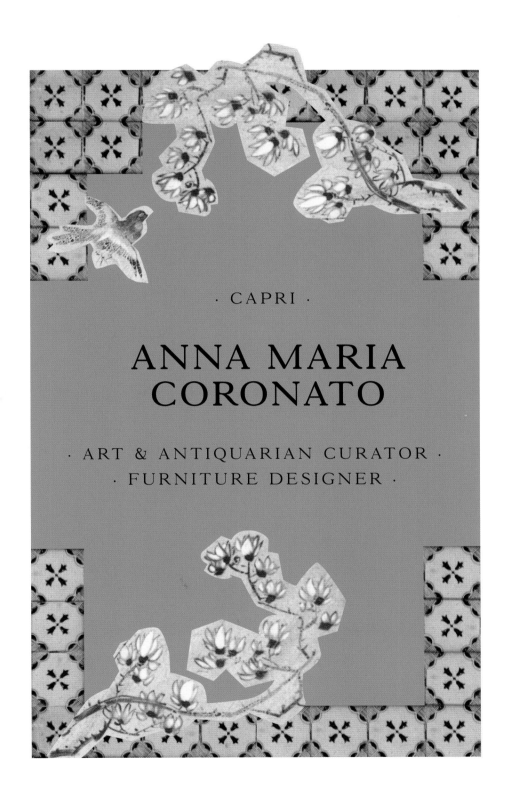

· CAPRI ·

ANNA MARIA CORONATO

· ART & ANTIQUARIAN CURATOR ·
· FURNITURE DESIGNER ·

Born in Italy in 1939, long-term Capri resident Anna Maria Coronato's dynamic career as an art and antiquarian specialist and furniture designer has spanned five decades and catapulted her from the private villas of Lazio and Liguria to the palaces of Rajasthan and beyond. Few things have provided her more inspiration, though, than Capri's historic homes and the imperial Roman ruins on her doorstep. The story of her life on the island provides us with a rare glimpse of a usually private world, like a wondrous missive from another time.

Capri's unique physical attributes have lured the wealthy and powerful for over 2000 years, ever since the Roman emperors began building enormous clifftop villas there. The structures' ancient remains captured Anna's childhood imagination, which was further fuelled by visits with her family to Villa le Scale, the Anacapri home of Baron Monti della Corte. Constructed in the early 1800s, the baron's whitewashed three-storey villa was threaded with a network of climbing jasmine and grapevines. Its six bedrooms (each with a terrace and sea views), expansive living areas and arched doorways and windows framing vistas to the Bay of Naples provided a secluded haven in the otherwise bustling summer locale. Among the many interior features that caught Anna's attention were the 18th-century majolica tiles from Vietri that covered the floors of the communal areas.

Anna's cultural education was further expanded in her home town of Naples, at her uncle's gallery of Roman antiquities and during excursions to the National Museum of Capodimonte. Set on around 130 hectares, the monumental pink and grey palazzo that houses the museum enraptured Anna when she first saw it as a fifteen-year-old. Its combination of historic interiors, priceless artworks and rare antique furniture left her 'awestruck not only by the vast number of 18th-century paintings but also the context in which they were displayed'. Along with its ballrooms and banquet halls, royal suites and rococo parlours, she discovered, among others, the work of Italian baroque painter Artemisia Gentileschi. Notable for her chiaroscuro works, Gentileschi surpassed in skill, power and message many of the great masters of the period.

It was the beauty of such interiors and artworks that drove Anna's desire to pursue tertiary education in the arts. In 1963, she completed her studies in art and Italian literature at the University of Florence; she subsequently took internships in the Old Masters departments of both Sotheby's and Christie's in London. She later opened private galleries in Rome and Naples, specialising in rare decorative objects, antiques and Neopolitan painting from the 18th century.

Anna and her late husband, Antonio D'Angelo, whom she met at a Neopolitan sailing club and whose family possesses 'the largest private collection of Neopolitan and Posillipo School 18th-century paintings in the world', created a life together centred around culture and creativity. 'My husband and I made a conscious choice not to have children. I always felt fulfilled by our relationship and my work,' Anna says. Following in the footsteps of their own families, they purchased a villa near the famed Grotta Azzurra and spent summers in Capri. In 1970, Anna opened Il Portico in Capri's Via Camerelle. A private gallery exhibiting art and rare antiques, it soon attracted a global clientele from the United States to India and the Middle East.

Meanwhile, the Capri of Anna's childhood was slowly disappearing. Many of the 18th- and early 19th-century homes had been demolished, and after the Monti della Corte family stopped visiting their villa, it fell into disrepair. When Anna was made aware of the situation, she became determined to save it and purchased the property in 1978.

— OPENING IMAGE
Exterior view of the uppermost tier of Villa le Scale, showing the stone-lined pool.

— OPPOSITE
A pergola-framed staircase leads to the villa's grand main entrance.

— FOLLOWING
The remaining foundations of Damecuta, one of Roman Emperor Tiberius's many Capri villas.

She restored it in stages, with much of the work done in 2002. Specialists built masonry vaults in several rooms, and artisans from Vietri painted tiles to match and replace those that were too badly damaged to restore. Museum-worthy pieces were installed to define each of the bedrooms, which were christened with corresponding names. 'The Venetian Room', for example, was named after a Venetian Empire chandelier hanging from the vaulted ceiling. 'The Louis XVI Room' featured boiserie wall panels along with an antique Louis XVI desk and chair, and masterworks from Anna's trove of 18th-century paintings were mounted in 'The Collectors' Room'.

Other rare and exotic objects were installed in the main living areas, including 19th-century crystal lamps from Rajasthan and a cluster of Moroccan pendant lamps in the dining room. On the main staircase landing, a 19th-century sculpture by French artist Roland Mathieu-Meusnier titled *The Death of Lais* was positioned to greet guests ascending to their bedrooms after supper. The work is a study for a larger version displayed in the Tuileries Garden in Paris.

Having been engulfed by weeds, the villa's extensive grounds required almost as much repair as the building itself. Only a handful of marine pine, fir and palm trees remained from the original garden. Anna took the opportunity to envisage an entirely new approach: 'I set about creating a "literary garden", with tiers of as many flowering plants and trees as the garden could hold.' For Anna, each flower and tree represented a code or metaphor, in much the same fashion as the literary gardens of the 17th and 18th centuries.

Once the restoration of Villa le Scale was complete, Anna used the home as a base for her frequent and extensive adventures scouring the world for unique treasures. In 2013, she opened a furniture and design gallery, KalaRara, with her business partner, Vincent Copeland. The multifaceted business includes the design of one-off tables and consoles handcrafted by local artisans, some of whom are also employed by the Vatican.

Along with the pieces designed and manufactured in their workshops, Anna and Vincent seek out distinctive antiques and modify them for modern living. One such find was a Tuscan neo-Gothic armoire from the 1890s with an intricately carved exterior. They refurbished the interior with a set of drawers lined with vintage Fornasetti wallpaper and two glass shelves were installed, as well as hidden lighting, to create a functional piece that marries tradition and modernity.

With hundreds of precious objects passing through Anna's galleries over more than half a century, she has become accustomed to letting them go. She takes a philosophical approach, considering herself a custodian of objects and artworks for future generations. She has a similar outlook regarding the many homes she has loved over her full and productive life, including Villa le Scale. Despite her strong affection for the property and extensive personal history there, she sold it a number of years ago.

Those wanting to follow in Anna's footsteps can rent the villa, fully staffed, during the warmer months for days or weeks at a time. After sightseeing among the island's imperial Roman ruins, guests might retire to the beautiful garden for an *aperitivo*, followed by a traditional Neopolitan or Caprese meal in the formal dining room — just as Anna did as a guest of Baron Monti della Corte more than seventy years ago.

† † †

— OPPOSITE
Via Krupp, a pedestrian pathway of hairpin turns, connects the Gardens of Augustus in Capri to the area known as Marina Piccola.

194

— CLOCKWISE FROM
TOP LEFT

— The Charterhouse of
Saint Giacomo, a nearby
14th-century Carthusian
monastery.

— Detail from a 19th-century
sculpture study for *Death of
Lais*, by French artist Roland
Mathieu-Meusnier.

— Detail of one of the villa's
guest bedrooms.

— A classical-style pergola
frames views of the Bay
of Naples near Capri's
main square.

— The island of Capri is
shrouded in myth and
wrapped in a skirt of
limestone and
dolomite cliffs.

— Antique drinks cabinet.

— Flowers and fruit from
the literary garden at
Villa le Scale.

· MELBOURNE ·

FIORINA &
FRANCESCA
GOLOTTA

FIORINA
JEWELLERY DESIGNER ·

FRANCESCA
· PHOTOGRAPHER ·

Ensconced in her bedroom in suburban Melbourne, threading shark's teeth and shells onto string to make herself a necklace, seven-year-old Fiorina Golotta embarked on a small creative project that marked the beginning of her life's work. Two years later, while accompanying her father, Tony, on a trip to his native Italy, the fate of her subsequent creative career was effectively sealed. The European history, architecture, art and jewellery she saw there made a profound impression, and the wildly contrasting aesthetic she found at Bangkok airport en route – 'Everything was shiny: mirrored beads, gold flowers and jewellery … it was phenomenal' – was equally intoxicating. By her tenth birthday she was fully accessorised in her own jewellery designs.

Not long after, Fiorina's younger sister Francesca had her own creative epiphany. On his forty-fifth birthday, Tony was given a coffee-table book, *Italia Mia*, featuring photographs by 1950s film-star-turned-photographer Gina Lollobrigida. Francesca pored over its pages of Italian street scenes and interiors and, encouraged by Fiorina, was soon experimenting with photography.

As Fiorina grew older, her creative work became inextricably linked to her sense of self. The handcrafted jewellery and talismans she made were not just objects of beauty and self-expression, but also tools of resistance. Tony, raised in poverty in conservative postwar southern Italy, wanted his children to pursue academic paths and corporate careers. So he saw his elder daughter's creative impulses as an expression of rebellion. Fiorina agreed. 'To be creative was a point of rebellion, an escape, an expression and a statement,' she explains. 'Jewellery made me feel uplifted, and it gave me an identity and an immediate shield.' It also exposed her to other ethnicities and cultures beyond the scope of her traditional upbringing, such as Native American groups, whose wisdom and protection she sought.

Fiorina left home at eighteen, a decision her parents did not welcome. Armed with freedom and independence for the first time, she discovered a different side of Melbourne, though was soon ready to move further afield. After throwing herself into a world of diverse ideologies and the underground music scene in New York City for a year, she returned to Australia and settled in the village of Kuranda in far-northern Queensland. There, she lost herself in a cathartic period of experimentation and self-development. Her new routine included working in an African bead shop, which offered her an informal education in tribal jewellery. 'African beads are not just decorative – they have a deeper cultural value. They are also religious, and some of them contain prayers,' she explains.

With a new sense of confidence in her creative needs and direction, fostered by several years of travel and exploration, she returned to Melbourne to study jewellery-making and started sharing a workshop in Little Collins Street. It was around this time that the sisters' parents divorced. 'It led us all to new paths,' says Francesca, 'and forged instant freedom. It meant we were no longer as engaged in the deep-rooted traditions of the Italian community.'

In 2003, when their father was terminally ill with cancer, Fiorina and her work were featured in a prominent magazine. A family friend visiting the bedridden Tony presented him with a laminated copy of the story. It was a defining moment of public recognition of Fiorina's work that made him incredibly proud. Similarly, the night before the hanging of Francesca and their brother Maurice's joint exhibition in 2002, they felt their father's enthusiasm. Francesca remembers: 'We were decorating these little icon frames

— OPENING IMAGE
Interior of Fiorina's boutique in the Melbourne suburb of Armadale.

— OPPOSITE
A detail from Fiorina's home office in Brighton, Melbourne.

— OPPOSITE
Fiorina and Francesca
among the coastal tea-trees
not far from the beach house
they share on the Mornington
Peninsula in Victoria.

we had made and nailing coins onto them that Fiorina had given us. Dad was going through chemotherapy at the time and feeling very unwell, and suddenly he came alive and insisted on showing us how we should do it.' As the exhibition opened, another chapter was coming to an end. There was not only new-found peace between Tony and his daughters but a celebration of all they had created.

In 2008, Fiorina and Francesca triumphantly opened Fiorina Jewellery on High Street Armadale. Its ornate golden doors open to an interior dotted with velvet chairs and antique mirrors, interspersed with polished cabinets displaying a magical array of handmade pieces. The walls feature Maurice's artwork and Francesca's photography. The workshop upstairs is the heart of the atelier, where all the jewellery is made. Tiny drawers are filled with a kaleidoscope of coloured gems and stones, and the collage-style decor includes evidence of Fiorina's travels, influences and interests.

Francesca's ability to be both the creative sounding board and the practical voice in the business continues to guide her sister, and Fiorina believes the differences between them are as important as their similarities. 'We're different people, and that's probably why it works,' she explains. 'Franca is a true Renaissance woman, she's romantic. I'm very fiery in comparison, and I learn from my mistakes afterwards. My aesthetic is more tribal and rustic, hers is more elegant and refined.'

These days, working with specific stones and materials continues to feed Fiorina's sense of wellbeing. 'The stones have power,' she says. 'It's about finding something that elevates you, something that helps you get through the day, the month, the year, the decade.' She finds the properties of stones potent: 'They give me the clarity needed to have the right thoughts, which lead to the right actions.'

Colour is also a significant driver in her life and work: 'I am attracted to certain colours for specific reasons. It's something I instinctively draw upon.' Turquoise is one example. 'Since my teens, I have been drawn to the traditional culture of people from those Native American nations that wear their hair long and employ turquoise jewellery, feathers and breastplates in their traditional dress, which gives them power and protection.' Similarly, the jewellery of the ancient Etruscan, Greek, Byzantine and Moghul cultures and traditional Art Deco aesthetics fascinate Fiorina. Her spiritual life is fed by these ancient cultures as well as Buddhism, mysticism and Rastafarianism. 'An appreciation of alternative ideologies has allowed me to embrace different ways of life, giving me creative freedom and providing a path forward.'

Looking back, Fiorina is philosophical about her upbringing: 'I believe you come into your family for a reason. My reason was about empowering and protecting people through what I do — through my jewellery.' Along with her prolific creative output, her rebellious tendencies also prepared her well for tackling the sometimes ruthless world of business.

Together, the sisters have created much more than a jewellery store. It is a focal point for like-minded women, a place they can go to feel inspired, adorned and understood. It has also provided Fiorina with an anchor: 'I think rebellion has been a curse and a blessing in the same breath. It steered the ship for a long time. The joy of creating and the response from my community, family and friends are now the primary driving forces in my life.'

† † †

— OPPOSITE AND ABOVE
The walls of the jewellery
workshop and design studio are
filled with drawings by Fiorina
and artworks by Francesca and
their brother, Maurice Golotta.

205

— CLOCKWISE FROM
BOTTOM LEFT

— Fiorina, wearing jewellery
of her own design.

— Fiorina's boutique in the
Melbourne suburb of Armadale.

— Fiorina's jewellery and
personal collections reflect
her spiritual connection with
the world around her.

— Fiorina collects old coins,
talismans, precious stones,
semi-precious beads
and vintage brooches and
often integrates them into
her designs.

— Fiorina's home office.

— Fiorina's jewellery designs
and beads for new pieces.

— A selection of bilums from
Fiorina's collection.

206

JESSICA GRINDSTAFF

· THEATRE DIRECTOR ·
· ARTIST ·

I f New York theatre director Jessica Grindstaff were to write a play based on her own life, the audience might assume that the unlikely plot was fiction. Her path to becoming an artist, set designer, creative director, theatre director and co-founder of the Phantom Limb Company in New York has been punctuated by experiences of crime, loss and displacement.

In 1977, her father robbed a bank in New Jersey; he was a heroin addict at the time and needed the money. Jessica's mother reported him to the police, and he was imprisoned just as Jessica's life was beginning. Their relationship was effectively over from the moment he was taken into custody; she never saw him again.

Jessica's mother changed their last name to ensure that he would not be able to find them, then remarried and moved several times before settling in Upstate New York. 'There was a narrative spun of this horrible, dangerous criminal – a violent man – all designed to keep me away from him,' Jessica explains.

With her elder half-sister often busy and their mother working, Jessica spent much of her time alone after school. She befriended the trees in a nearby forest and began building makeshift structures from natural materials to create performances. Plants and birds were often her only audience, but, looking back, those experiences 'creating a world from nothing' provided her with a toolkit for her later work.

By age fourteen, Jessica's relationship with her mother was fractured and the situation at home had become untenable. She was placed in foster care with Dana and Mel Toomey, whom she had known from birth – years earlier, they had also provided care for her mother. While they were not blood relatives, the Toomeys were Jessica's chosen grandparents and being with them fed her personal development and cultural awareness. Dana's career in education and advocacy, healing and art had begun in her early twenties, when she danced professionally in New York City. She shared her love of performance with Jessica, taking her to shows and encouraging her to interpret them through an intuitive and emotive lens.

Through her understanding of disciplines such as Ayurveda, neuromuscular therapy, Pilates, traditional Chinese medicine and medical qi gong, Dana also helped Jessica heal. And Mel's background as one of the founders of the leadership coaching and change management movement in the US made him more than qualified to advise and encourage Jessica. She describes him as her 'lifelong intellectual and emotional coach'.

Dana and Mel also helped find Jessica a new school that supported her interest in the visual arts. The Buxton School in Williamstown, Massachusetts, nestled in the mountains against the backdrop of the Taconic Ridge State Forest, was the perfect fit. Jessica says, 'In my free time, I went to the nearby pastures or woods or to the Clark Art Institute,' which has one of the best small art collections in New England.

Dominating the lobby of the Clark was a large work in oil, *Fumée d'ambre gris* (Smoke of ambergris), by John Singer Sargent. Orientalist in feel, it features a woman holding part of her costume over her head to capture the perfume of smoking ambergris in a silver censer. It became Jessica's favourite painting, and she liked to sit on a bench nearby, happily hypnotised. Years later, the work inspired the costume design in her first major theatre production.

After completing high school, and while trudging through several unsatisfying years of tertiary study in Massachusetts, Jessica met musician and composer Erik Sanko when his band, Skeleton Key, came to perform. Learning that he was not only a musician and composer but also had a secret obsession with puppet-making, Jessica asked to make a documentary about him for an assignment. During the long days in the editing room, she fell in love with him.

— OPENING IMAGE
Jessica Grindstaff with her daughter Freya.

— OPPOSITE
The home of Jessica's youth was designed and built in the late 1970s by Robert Hillier & Associates in conjunction with Dana and Mel Toomey.

— OPPOSITE
Jessica and Freya at the
Toomeys' home in Connecticut.
Dana's sculptures are displayed
throughout the home,
including above the fireplace.
Building was completed in
1979, the year after Jessica was
born, and she describes the
home as 'the only constant
I have ever known'.

In 2000, when Jessica was twenty-two, they married. Soon, they were collaborating on new projects, including a joint exhibition of Jessica's dioramas and Erik's puppets at the Debora Gallery in Greenpoint, Brooklyn. In a post-9/11 atmosphere of fear and foreboding, the simple human stories incorporating lovingly handmade artworks were a tonic.

Their first full-length theatre production, *The Fortune Teller*, followed soon after, at the cutting-edge HERE Arts Center in Soho in 2006. Unable to find a set designer, Jessica stepped into the role: 'I was already making these little worlds and dioramas, so I figured the sets would just be bigger versions of the same.' They played to a full house every night and the three-week season extended to three months, cementing their reputation among the downtown avant-garde.

In 2007, the Phantom Limb Company was born. Jessica and Erik continue to follow their instincts and are not constrained by the history or tradition of puppet theatre. Instead, they experiment with innovative ways of operating their marionettes. While the puppets drive the main narrative, each show also utilises multiple other art forms, including photography, film, mask, installation and dance.

For Jessica, their work is a form of activism. She believes that stories about climate and social change shared through individual human experiences can be effectively communicated through art and theatre. Over the past decade, Phantom Limb has created a trilogy to convey stories of adversity, leadership, endurance and survival. The overarching goal is to highlight 'people's relationship to the environment and climate change through poetic narratives'. Part 1 of the trilogy explores Ernest Shackleton's doomed 1914 Imperial Trans-Antarctic Expedition; Part 2 tells the story of one of the world's oldest living trees, a Great Basin bristlecone called Methuselah; and Part 3 offers hope after the Fukushima tsunami and the Daiichi and Daini nuclear power plant disasters of 2011.

While creating visual narratives in her work, Jessica has been simultaneously dealing with unexpected changes to her personal story. Growing up, she believed her father had never attempted to contact her, but she recently discovered this was not the case. 'He had requested contact through a judge in order to try to maintain a relationship,' she explains, 'and my mother refused.' After her father died, her mother sent Jessica a link to the Facebook page of a young man, along with the message: 'I think this might be your brother.' Looking through his photos online, Jessica recognised something of herself: 'In all of his photographs, he was smiling with his mouth closed. And I said to Erik, "I'm going to find a candid picture of him, and I'll bet you anything he has my teeth!" My whole life I've smiled with my mouth closed because I'm embarrassed by them. Sure enough, we went through fifty photos and saw one goofy smile. The exact same teeth! So I wrote to him and said, "I think we might be related".'

In 2015, she began the process of getting to know her late father through her three newly discovered half-siblings. The first time they met, Jessica asked if they would share some happy memories of their father with her. 'What they all said was that his pride in them was so overwhelming, that they felt like they were the smartest, most interesting and most fantastic kids in the world. Which was beautiful to hear but also really hard, because I didn't have that in my childhood.'

It's easy to imagine, though, that if Jessica could spend time with her father now, he would think that she too was one of the smartest, most interesting and most fantastic people in the world.

† † †

— ABOVE

Rabbits and hand-carved
wooden blocks inside Freya's
bedroom in the family's
Tribeca apartment.

— OPPOSITE

Paper-mâché puppets made by
Jessica's husband Erik Sanko
for their work 69°S.

214

— CLOCKWISE FROM
TOP LEFT

— Jessica's workstation,
framed by her paintings and
dioramas, in the New York
studio she shares with Erik.

— One of Jessica's dioramas in
their Tribeca apartment.

— The master bedroom in
Jessica and Erik's apartment.

— Detail with piano
and collected treasures in
Freya's bedroom.

— Jessica and Dana by
Woodridge Lake on the
Toomeys' property.

— Detail of wooden figure
inside the master bedroom
of their Tribeca apartment.

— Freya negotiates the
same stone pathway on the
Toomeys' property that Jessica
walked as a child.

216

NEW YORK ·

PETAH COYNE

· ARTIST ·

Before the guests arrived at their Hawaiian home, five-year-old Petah Coyne and her siblings were issued with clear instructions: move quietly and slowly. Their father, Bob Coyne, a US military man, had invited a number of World War II veterans over for a barbecue. The men had survived the Bataan Death March of 1942 but had lost, among other things, their ability to engage in normal conversation and continued to be easily startled by noise and sudden movement.

Intermittent visits by the veterans left a deep impression on Petah. 'They would just sit there, because they wanted to be around life but couldn't quite get back into it,' she recalls. She wished she could help them, and creative visualisations gave form to her feelings. 'I used to sit near their chairs and pretend I was tethering them to the Earth, because I felt that without my help they would just lift off and fly up into the sky.'

Bob was a military doctor and he and his family were required to relocate often. They averaged a move a year, but sometimes it was more frequent. Petah was born in Oklahoma City in 1953, and before she was twelve, the family had moved fifteen times. The place that left the most profound impression on her, which at four years was also one of Bob's longest postings, was Oahu, Hawaii, where they lived in a Japanese enclave. She felt an immediate affinity for Japanese culture, and the cultural traditions and experiences she was exposed to during that period helped lay the foundations for her to become one of New York's most highly respected and important artists.

Many of the lessons Petah learned in Hawaii were not taught at school. She was introduced, for example, to meditation under the guidance of an elderly Japanese woman, Mama Doi, who lived across the road from Petah's family. 'She would take me by the hand and say, "Now we are going to sit in my garden and we are going to watch the garden grow",' Petah explains. The practice helped her to quieten her body and mind for long enough to fully see and appreciate the forms and colours of nature.

The small, self-contained community was also embraced by Petah's mother, Bobbie, who rejected some of the classic pursuits of American women in the 1950s in favour of those enjoyed by the Japanese. She began studying *ikebana*, and the whole family assisted with lengthy foraging missions on beaches and in the woods on weekends, searching for interesting organic objects to use in her work. After her mother had placed a number of the elements together in an arrangement, she would sit her children on stools around the table and ask them to share their thoughts. If their hands shot up quickly, she would say, 'Not so fast', then proceed to slowly swivel the base of the arrangement and urge them to contemplate the composition from all sides. Petah now recognises that she was being schooled in the art of sculpture and, coupled with Mama Doi's teachings, in the art of seeing.

Flowers are a childhood motif omnipresent in Petah's work today. As well as featuring in Mama Doi's garden and her mother's ikebana arrangements, they flourished in Hawaii's tropical climate. As Petah says, 'We had orchids and gardenias everywhere. My mother would pick them and wear them on her dresses, and we would make traditional flower garlands.'

In testament to her ongoing fascination with flowers in their myriad forms, a large section of Petah's New Jersey studio is dedicated to the preparation of blooms to use in her work. Like a magical indoor garden with flourishing flowerbeds, hundreds of silk blossoms are organised by type and colour on long benches, awaiting artistic anointment. There are clusters of blooms in a spectrum of hues and tones, from cherry red and aubergine to matte black and whispering white. Each flower has either been lightly coated in paint or dipped

— **OPENING IMAGE**
Portrait of Petah Coyne.

— **OPPOSITE**
Sculpture by Petah Coyne, *Untitled #1375 (No Reason Except Love: Portrait of a Marriage)*, 2011–12.

— PREVIOUS
A work in progress inside the
artist's private studio.

— OPPOSITE
View from the window of
Petah Coyne's apartment in
New York City.

in a specially formulated and patented wax for use in one of Petah's installations. Several of her finished works hang like oversized chandeliers from the studio ceiling, while others seem to flow across the floor in a lava-like disgorging of creative juices.

The natural world evokes in Petah an array of conflicting emotions, from joy and fascination to fear and dread. Her father was a passionate deep-sea diver and would return home after diving expeditions with seabed treasures for Petah and her siblings. His love of the ocean turned to terror, however, on one diving trip with a close friend who was attacked by a shark and died. Bob never went diving again, and upon learning the news, Petah developed a fear of the surf. 'What you find in nature is so much scarier than the stuff in monster movies,' she says. 'I was very frightened by nature. I knew it was very dangerous, but I also loved it.'

Petah's early work often featured detritus that she would mine from swamps and dry to use in her sculptures. 'I find the sculptural forms in nature fascinating — anthills, beehives, termite mounds, molehills and animal habitats of all types,' she says.

Petah has created her own personal habitat in Soho, New York. Perhaps one of the consequences of relocating so often as a child is that she has chosen to stay in the same apartment for her entire adult life. She lives there with her husband, Lamar Hall, whom she met at school.

A great believer in the importance of cultural rituals for the health of communities, and daily rituals and routines for the wellbeing of the individual, the structure of Petah's days is thoughtfully considered. She wakes at 4 am to meditate or read for several hours in her book-lined apartment, and then heads to her studio while most New Yorkers are still in bed. Her unshakeable discipline and singular focus combined with her rich inner story and unique imagination have resulted in the creation of works that have been collected by more than fifty major art museums. These include New York's Museum of Modern Art, Solomon R Guggenheim Museum, the Metropolitan Museum of Art, the Whitney Museum of American Art and the Smithsonian Institution in Washington, DC.

Petah's work draws on not only the natural world but also infamous female characters in cinema, Southern Gothic and feminist literature, and Japanese embroidered kimonos, among other things. Materials for her are like letters or words from a secret language and include everything from chicken wire, glass, satin ribbons and hand-sewn velvet to organic matter such as mud, human hair, tree branches and taxidermied peacocks and geese.

As vital as the world that inspires her, Petah is an artist who lives each day with vigour and passion, her work reflecting meaningful connections with multiple cultures and an abiding concern for the Earth. Her oeuvre sings a hymn of reverence to women and nature, inviting our consideration and perhaps even helping to inspire our joint action.

† † †

— CLOCKWISE FROM
BOTTOM LEFT

— Petah's home library.

— Petah Coyne, *Untitled #778
(Honolulu)*, 1994.

— Waxed and unwaxed flowers
in preparation to be used in
one of Petah's works.

— Petah Coyne, *Untitled #1336
(Scalapino Nu Shu)*, 2009–10.

— Tools and brushes in
the studio.

— Red waxed orchids ready
for use in one of Petah's
sculptures and, to the left,
small waxed hands.

· YUCATÁN, MEXICO ·

DEV STERN

· CULTURAL
AMBASSADOR ·

A t the wheel of the family station wagon with wife Alice beside him, John Milloy pulled away from the curb, ready for another Mexican adventure. Their six children, including youngest girls Dorothea and Janet, were piled in the back. Ciudad Valles and the Hotel Covadonga were ahead on the distant horizon.

With its long, shady verandahs, verdant grounds and excellent cuisine, the hotel was the epitome of tropical bliss. Seated in the dining room, guests could enjoy views of clipped lawns and an attractive golf course through the oversized arched windows, while friendly staff helped them feel at home. Of all the family's holidays in Mexico, it was the food, service and gardens at the Hotel Covadonga that most captured Dorothea's imagination.

Born in North Carolina in 1955 and raised in Texas, she displayed an early penchant for unorthodox adventures. As a child, her escapades led the family to dub her 'Diablo', though it was the English translation, 'Devil', that stuck. Decades later, at the request of her mother-in-law (who hoped she might change her name for the sake of respectability), she shortened Devil to Dev, and has been known by that name ever since.

Like Dev, Charles 'Chuck' Stern's childhood was lived between Texas and Mexico. When they met as undergraduates in 1974, they found they had much in common; they married five years later. In 1995, after 'continued treks to Mexico, exploring old and new backroads' with their son, Evan, in tow, they began to look for a property to buy. Four years later, a chance encounter with Karen Witynski, who, with her husband, Joe Carr, had written several books on Mexican architecture and interiors, directed their attention to the south-eastern state of Yucatán.

When they pulled up at the 400-year-old Hacienda Petac, a crumbling Spanish colonial estate set on 100 hectares, something resonated. Though 'the grounds were a barren moonscape of limestone', there was ample groundwater, which gave them hope that the desolate landscape could be transformed. Their enthusiasm was tempered, however, when they struggled to find a like-minded architect and builder to restore the property. Hopes near-dashed, they at last met architect Salvador Reyes Rios and his design partner and wife, Josefina Larrain. Locals from the nearby city of Mérida, they shared Dev and Chuck's passion for the hacienda's 17th-century architecture and their desire to resurrect the site.

They also shared an interest in ancient Mayan culture, evidence of which could still be found on the property. For Dev, the property's complex history came with a great sense of responsibility, as 'the estate was built for the Spaniards using stones they'd plundered from the Mayans'. The irony of being foreigners 'reclaiming' traditional Mayan land was not lost on Dev, who saw in 'the abandoned footprints of a thriving Mayan community... a reminder that we are merely following shadows on this land and are custodians more than owners'.

With the site's history at front of mind, Salvador and Josefina went to work. They soon discovered the traditional stucco finishes buried beneath the ruins of the hacienda, which revealed the walls' original colours and textures. The next step was to find artisans who knew how to create similar results — not an easy task, as many of the ancient building techniques were no longer practised. However, Salvador assembled a team of local masons and resurrected an old stucco recipe that combined natural resin from native chukum trees with Yucatecan lime. The finish was authentic, impermeable and durable, as well as aesthetically pleasing, with a soft textural quality and subtle earthy tone.

The extensive works involved rebuilding the roofs and walls and repairing the Moorish arches that punctuate the facade of the main house and frame its stone-paved terraces. Seven bedrooms, complete with ensuite bathrooms with polished native-stone showers and baths, were created along with a large games room. The builders refitted

— OPENING IMAGE
The main dining room in Hacienda Petac.

— OPPOSITE
The kitchen of the *Casa Principal* (main house), showing the hand-carved *copete*, or crest.

— OPPOSITE
One of many shady areas in the hacienda's extensive grounds.

— FOLLOWING FROM LEFT
— The front verandah of the Casa Principal, leading to the hacienda's main dining room.
— The covered veranda of the Casa de Maquinas, leading to the spacious Chun Jun bedroom.

traditional wooden ceiling beams in several rooms and painted them to contrast with the wall colours. Ochre hues were chosen for the dining room and kitchen, soft mustard for the chapel and cornflower blue for the tiny prayer room.

In keeping with local traditions, the team also made extensive use of tiles for practical and decorative purposes. They repaired or replaced the soft-green tiles on the floors of the large dining room, living room and library, and used blue and white talavera clay and ceramic tiles in the kitchen. A hand-carved wooden *copete* (crest) was chosen for the wall above the cooktop and a large wooden table was installed as the kitchen's centrepiece. Other furniture was made by local artisans or was custom-designed by Salvador and Josefina, including a collection of butaca-style rocking chairs in wood and leather, and Yucatecan antiques were sourced by Karen and Joe.

Landscaping was of paramount importance to Dev and Chuck, and to oversee the design they enlisted the services of American landscape architect and friend Sam Fallis. His plan included a series of winding pathways that would lead through dense foliage of coconut, banana and mango trees. The property's gates were repaired along with the driveway, which led past a series of flame trees to the main house. The hacienda's chimney, evidence of the property's former life as a henequen factory, was reimagined as a tranquil water feature with what appear to be floating rocks set across a rectangular pool, while a large water tank made way for a swimming pool framed by tropical plants and strung with hammocks.

In June 2002, with the restoration almost complete but significantly over budget, Dev and Chuck decided that as well as using the hacienda for their own extended family and friends, they would make it available for private rental. That meant finding and hiring staff from the local village, Petac, which brought its own set of challenges. During the training process, Dev realised that a lifetime of travel in Mexico hadn't prepared her for the linguistic, cultural and economic differences she found.

In September 2002, just months before the first paying guests were due to arrive and only weeks after building works had been completed, word spread that Hurricane Isidore was headed in their direction. Staff helped Dev secure the property before the storm hit and she sheltered in one of the guest rooms for the duration. Despite over half a million local people being left homeless and essential services being badly damaged, Dev was spared the worst. In a stroke of luck, a large falling tree was caught by a second tree, effectively saving the building, and with it, Dev's life. In the clean-up, Dev and the villagers worked with a shared vision to repair Petac's homes as well as the hacienda and its garden.

Once repairs were completed, Dev was left with one major unsolved problem: she needed a cook with a traditional Yucatecan background. They searched for someone who would be an artful exponent of the local culinary culture and able to train the kitchen staff on how to prepare regional recipes. After months of trial and error, Dev was introduced to Doña Mari, a local village elder with a deep knowledge of traditional Yucatecan cooking, which has Cuban, Spanish and Mayan influences. Doña Mari and the women who followed in her footsteps brought a wonderful art to the kitchen, creating an atmosphere of pride and enjoyment that spilled into the food. Over the years, guests became so enamoured with the hacienda's cuisine that, in 2014, Dev opened a traditional Yucatecan cooking school on the premises.

At the end of each day, guests are treated to cocktails followed by formal dinner. No part of the dining experience at Hacienda Petac is overlooked, right down to the traditional staff uniforms — hand-embroidered linen dresses made by local women. Dev wants visitors to feel that each meal is a special occasion. With Hacienda Petac, she has created a spiritual, cultural and culinary haven for all to enjoy.

† † †

— CLOCKWISE FROM
BOTTOM LEFT

— A handmade stool
traditionally used when
making tortillas.

— The Toh twin bedroom,
located in the *Casa de Maquinas*,
is named for the Toh bird,
whose song can often be heard
on the hacienda's grounds.

— The 'floating rocks' at the
base of the hacienda's 60-foot
former factory chimney, which
is now a tranquil water feature.
It was built 200 years ago as
part of the exhaust system for
the steam-engine operated
machinery used to process
henequen and sisal for export.

— The small early 19th-century
chapel, *La Capilla de San
Antonio*, located on the
hacienda grounds, is also used
by residents of the local village.

— View across the 19th-century
tiled floor to the entrance of
La Capilla de San Antonio.

— Mangoes and decorative
seeds from a Mexican palm
tree in a wooden barrel in
the kitchen.

— View to the garden through
an early 17th-century
Islamic-style arch.

· ACKNOWLEDGEMENTS ·

– OPPOSITE
The garden pathway that leads to the citrus groves of the Marchesi di San Guiliano farm in Sicily. The grounds of the property provide Fiona Corsini with infinite inspiration for her paintings.

Thank you to the following people who have advised on, assisted with or encouraged me during the course of this project:

Firstly, to the inspiring and talented women who are featured in these pages, along with your partners and families. You welcomed me into your private homes and studios, and it is due to your trust, openness and generosity that this book has come to life. I am enormously grateful to you all.

To Marina Cukeric, Jo Yeldham, Heidi Middleton and Amber and Camilla Guinness, who made suggestions or provided introductions to potential subjects for the project. And to the friends who offered personal encouragement, insight and support: Penelope Scott, Sabina Reid, Josephine Corcoran, Caroline Cox, Rebecca Ascher, Mike and Mim Bartlett, Nicola Lester, Garth Davis, Concetta Maulucci, Anna A'Beckett, Andrew Stephens, Nathalie Kemp, Bec Cole, Matthew Smith, Seri Renkin and Nicola Granter. With special thanks to Lyn and Richard Lea, for helping with the text and general advice and ideas, and Sally Balharrie, for providing creative coaching right when I needed it.

To Andy Quin, for helping with production on many levels; you're a joy to work with and you make it all so much more fun. And to Barbara Marsiletti and Emanuele Tortona, for helping me photograph JJ Martin's apartment in Milan for the book's cover. All via Zoom!

To Katrina Dowd from Domestic Textiles Corporation, for kindly sharing the company's beautiful fabrics and wallpapers for several of our shoots, including Lucette by Paloma Wallpaper and Jaipir and Evelyn fabric by Zoffany.

To all those who provided help in other important ways: Colleen Leonard, Martha Morano, Oshoke Pamela Abalu, Dana and Mel Toomey, Erik Sanko, Prince Filippo and Princess Giorgiana Corsini, Benjamin Ashworth, Vincent Copeland, Chelsey VanderVliet, Luca Zappa, Jason McCoy, Silvia Mariotti, Jessica Maliszewski, Willam Roper-Curzon, Julia and Tanya Lea, Lucia Turegano, Bradley Seymour, Emma Wright-Smith, Carly Rowell, Brydie Kelliher, Pierre Imhof, Gilles Massé, David and Marie-Therese Hunt, Alfred Liechtenstein, Matthew Bell, Lucrezia and Luna Bonaccorsi Beccaria, Sara Agostoni, Arabella Ruffo, Francesca Parini, Edward and Marina Lambton, Duccio Corsini and Clotilde Trentinaglia de Daverio.

To Ashlea O'Neill for all the work you put into designing this tome, and to Katie Purvis and Sam Palfreyman for your diligent and fine editing skills and ongoing support.

To Kirsten Abbott, and the entire team at Thames and Hudson. Not only for commissioning the book but for your guidance, enthusiasm and encouragement during the course of the project.

To my husband, Tim. I am so appreciative that you took the time to read the chapters in progress and for your honest feedback, ongoing love and encouragement – it means the world to me. And to our children, Freddie and Issy: being twelve and fourteen, you are now old enough to form and articulate your own views, which I have loved hearing while creating this book.

To Sara Benn, my mentor and muse. While you are no longer around to discuss and dissect projects such as these, your artistry, playfulness and expansive spirit will continue to inspire what I do. I miss you terribly, think of you every day and dedicate this book to you.

† † †

First published in Australia in 2021
by Thames & Hudson Australia Pty Ltd
11 Central Boulevard, Portside Business Park
Port Melbourne, Victoria 3207
ABN: 72 004 751 964

First published in the United Kingdom in 2021
By Thames & Hudson Ltd
181a High Holborn
London WC1V 7QX

First published in the United States of America in 2021
By Thames & Hudson Inc.
500 Fifth Avenue
New York, New York 10110

Thames & Hudson Australia wishes to acknowledge that Aboriginal and
Torres Strait Islander people are the first storytellers of this nation
and the traditional custodians of the land on which we live and work.
We acknowledge their continuing culture and pay respect to Elders
past, present and future.

ISBN 978-1-760-76039-7
ISBN 978-1-760-76174-5 (U.S. edition)

A catalogue record for this
book is available from the
National Library of Australia

British Library Cataloguing-in-Publication Data
A catalogue record for this book is available from the British Library

Library of Congress Control Number 2020947024

Be the first to know about our new releases,
exclusive content and author events by visiting
thamesandhudson.com.au
thamesandhudson.com
thamesandhudsonusa.com

FSC® is dedicated to the promotion of responsible forest management
worldwide. This book is made of material from FSC®-certified forests and
other controlled sources.